*Achieve Sharp Emotional Awareness
and Clarity, Quickly & Easily!*

Emotional

Awareness

Uncommon Sense about
Everyday Feelings

*"You're going to <u>LOVE</u>
how you feel!"*

Dr. John S. Nagy

Emotional Awareness *Made Easy*

Uncommon Sense about Everyday Feelings

Publisher: Promethean Genesis Publishing
PO Box 636
Lutz FL 33548-0636

ISBN-10: 0-9793070-1-5
ISBN-13: 978-0-9793070-1-0

First Printing, August 2008
Published in the United States of America
Book edited by Arthur Cornett and Dr. John S. Nagy
Illustrations by Dr. John S. Nagy

Book available at: www.coach.net and www.provokingsuccess.com

The author is available for speaking, workshop and coaching engagements. Please contact him through his websites listed above or by calling 813-949-0718.

Emotional Awareness *Made Easy*

<u>Dedication</u>

To my wife, my sons and my friends.
You've all shown me so much about
how I perceive the world
and I am richer for this.

To all who venture forth and quest to refine and expand your
abilities. May you find greater awareness, ability and success
because of your grand thoughts.

<u>Acknowledgements</u>

A heartfelt thanks to the countless dictionaries, thesauruses,
websites, search engines and friendly contributions that have
helped me create the cumulative lists of emotions contained within
this book.

<u>Disclaimer</u>

This book is not a substitute for professional help. Please do not
use it with that intention.

Please seek a professional trained to assist you with your specific
challenge if you have experienced trauma, suffer from Post
Traumatic Stress Syndrome, experience non-ordinary emotional
issues or Emotional Abuse.

Introduction

For a very long time the Star Trek character "Spock" was a hero of mine. Through naïve eyes, I saw him as cool, calm and collected – nearly nothing ever upset him. I struggled with emotions; he didn't. His unruffled use of logic and his blatant dismissal of emotions was a positive draw for me. I idolized him for years and held him up as a standard for how I should react to emotions as a male. Like many other men, I was uneducated in the importance and purposes of emotions. I believed, like him, that emotions were not necessary and that they actually interfered with living life.

Emotions were very elusive and uncontrolled creatures to me. I knew they were present but I didn't know why or what they said. *Many times, I totally missed the entire underlying message emotions shared.* They didn't make sense to me. When they were noticeable, things always quickly got out of hand. I liked to believe that I could dismiss them so that then I wouldn't have to deal with them. I didn't realize how much I was missing because of that belief.

What made things worse is that other people seemed to know more about my emotions than I did. These people always left me feeling at a disadvantage in many social situations. I liked this least of all. It wasn't until I reached my mid 30s that I came to realize what emotions actually were. What I discovered was awesome and my world opened up. I started to understand much more about emotions and what that knowledge could do for me than I ever imagined possible. Even Mr. Spock would have been shocked!

In many ways, the book you're reading represents a written record of my accumulated discoveries and progression understanding of

emotions. I bared the basics. I found the fallacies and falsehoods. I learned how to grasp what emotions truly were, what they weren't and what they could tell me.

My quest for knowledge paid off. My emotions revealed to me their purposes for being a part of our unique human makeup. They showed me how they could empower me to more fully affirm my life. I learned how they gave me great advantage in dealing with life much more effectively. In short, I benefited immensely.

I also realized that what had been given to me was too important to keep to myself. I wanted earnestly to share what I had learned with others, especially those who could benefit most. This book was the cumulative result of that desire.

As I put this book together, my purpose was clear-cut:
Create an opportunity for readers to take an empowering look at emotions which can improve their awareness, their choices and their lives.

To accomplish this, I have made effort to provoke new understanding in the reader very much like it occurred for me. In doing so, I have made effort to offer simple explanations and provide supporting examples that make sense. I have provided methods and exercises for applying this information, in the hope that this book could make a significant difference for the reader. *Otherwise, there would be no point in providing all this information if it could not be applied for benefit.*

Only after this book was nearly completed did I realize the tremendous need for improving emotional awareness in both our professional and personal lives.

A book designed to _quickly develop emotional clarity, insight, understanding and communication_ would help. A book filled with frank information designed to empower the reader – *you* – to better understand, what occurs for you both inside and outside might even be a blessing. I know it was for me.

When I look back over what I've written here, I reflect again on Mr. Spock, one of the heroes of my youth. I imagine his response to my efforts. I believe he would say that sharing this book was the only *logical* thing to do.

I hope that within these pages you'll find what you need to empower you to improve both your emotional awareness and your future success. May your life be richer for your efforts!

Exploration Opportunity:

1. *Visualize your gain!* Ask yourself what you would like to obtain by reading this book.

2. *Write this down!* You can review it once you have completed reading this book to see if you got what you wanted.

3. *Get more!* To maximize your *return on investment* in this book, read "**Make the Most of This Book**" located on pages 162 and 163 in the "Index Section" of this book!

3

I. Tune In – Awareness!

*When the radio station broadcasts
but your radio is not tuned in,
all you ever hear is static.*

*Turning off your radio
Without trying to tune in
is not the best solution
to a static situation.*

*Once you've tuned in, you can
understand and enjoy
so much more.*

***

*Awareness is a vigilantly conscious effort
to remain open to new information
about your changing situations.*

*To be aware,
you must commit to excellence.*

Brace Yourself for a Paradigm Shift

*There are times when you finally arrive at where you thought you
wanted to be only to realize that the transformation you truly
achieved was in how you look at things.*

A paradigm is a map that helps you understand a certain territory;
however, they're not the
territory themselves. What
they do is present to
travelers of such territories
useful models that aid
them in grasping and
dealing more effectively
with the realities of these
territories. *They also
strongly influence and
dictate how travelers
perceive these terrains.*

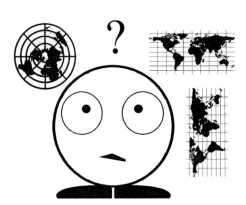

Most people have one basic emotional paradigm. They believe
emotions are *energies that dwell within, they have a mind of their
own* and *there is little that one can do about them.* Based on this
paradigm, many actions people take are usually done *to minimize
the damage emotions cause* and *to have these energies run their
course in the hope that things may eventually return to "normal."*

What you are reading now is a new map of *your* emotional
territory. It'll challenge and hopefully *transform your
preconceived notions* about what emotions are and aren't, what
they do and don't do, and why and how they do the things they do.
When you complete this book, you'll have an entirely new way to
understand, view and perhaps even experience emotions – *one that
can transform your life for the better.*

So much more becomes possible with paradigm shifts.

A. Getting to Know Your Tuner

Q: What does your tuner look like?

A: Just look at the image bouncing back at you from the mirror and you'll know!

You *are* your tuner and if that surprises you then it's probably a worthwhile idea to familiarize yourself with some basics before you start making effort toward tuning in.

COMPONENTS OF EMOTIONS

Your tuner is comprised of three distinct components, which are mental, physical & behavioral in nature.

MENTAL

The mental component of your tuner is your thoughts. Specifically it's how you think and what you believe about your situation. Your perception determines which emotion your body produces. Many factors influence your thoughts, including (but not limited to) personal values, intentions, perceptions, paradigms and experiences. Each of these can occur in a several forms.

PHYSICAL

The physical component of emotion consists of the various changes that occur within the body simultaneously with the emotion. Emotions affect body chemistry, memory and function,

6

which in turn are sensed by the body. *These sensed changes are not the emotions.* These changes are the shift in your body's energy patterns caused by the emotions. When the body produces little or no significant changes, the intensity of the emotion is less. The more sensitive you are to these kinds of change in your energy patterns, the more you'll feel the impact of your emotions.

BEHAVIORAL

The behavioral component includes your visible, auditory and kinesthetic emotional expression. You show these behaviors through facial expressions, gestures (both overt and subtle) and posture. Also included are your vocal tones and your choice of words. Finally, add to this how you: touch, respond to touch, and move your body in response to a given situation, and you have the outward signs of what is occurring internally.

…

This book focuses on helping you increase your awareness of each component, what occurs for each one specifically and consciously put all three components together, as well as how each one impacts the others. It is hoped that this will empower you to make better choices overall and have them collectively benefit you into the future.

B. Emotional Illusions

Your perceptions can fool you.

No matter how you might try to be "reality" based, events in your life can mislead you into thinking that something is true when, upon further examination, you find that it is clearly false.

Example: When you look at the picture on this page, at first glance, the two clusters appear to be different sizes. One appears to be larger. Still, upon further examination, you will see that the center circles are actually identical in size. This picture is an illusion created by what surrounds them. The conditions that exist around each of these two identical circles give the impression that they 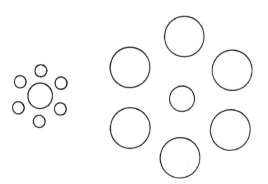 are of different sizes. Had you not examined them further, you might have believed that the center circles where dissimilar in size.

Much like our perceptions of these two circles, emotions frequently present themselves surrounded by all sorts of differing conditions that give impressions that mislead. Without a closer look, you can act upon these misleading impressions as you navigate through life. If you make a choice based on the wrong information, you're bound to travel down the wrong path. This is not effective and can often be harmful. If you want to be on a path that produces the results you desire, you have to make choices supportive of this. Knowing more about emotions can help you do exactly that.

Without a doubt, false information affects your perception. It's important to know these falsehoods before you make any efforts to tune in.

Here's a *quick quiz* offered to you to see how aware you are about some common falsehoods brought about by illusions.

POP QUIZ

Which statements below are false?

1. *My emotions are feelings.*
2. *At times, someone else can control my emotions.*
3. *Sometimes I'm not responsible for how I'm feeling.*
4. *If I say, "I am angry" and mean it, it's true.*
5. *I can feel good or bad.*
6. *I have positive & negative emotions to deal with.*
7. *Emotions are irrational and illogical.*
8. *Emotions are a problem for others and me.*
9. *At times, I think it is wrong to feel a certain way.*
10. *Sometimes I think it's wimpy to show emotions.*
11. *Only women have emotional cycles.*
12. *Emotions are energy.*

Knowing which of these statements are false is important in order for emotional awareness to be accurate and be of benefit to you. Believing a fallacy to be true leads you to make choices under false pretenses. As a result, you'll be less likely to realize the outcomes you truly desire.

Let's look at each of these 12 statements more carefully:

1. Feelings are Not Emotions

Believe it or not, body sensations are not emotions!

When you think that you "feel" an emotion, you're really feeling the effect of that emotion and not the emotion itself.

This "feeling" sensation occurs because emotions shift your body's energy. That shift causes a myriad of body sensations.

Example #1: *You experience fear. You feel all the usual body sensations that you would expect when this emotion occurs. You then perceive the danger that was present is no longer relevant and you experience **relief**. All the usual body sensations associated with fear now shift to body sensations associated with relief. This is because each emotion creates different associated shifts and hence different associated sensations.*

You might be tempted though to think that the sensations *are* the emotions. *This is an illusion. These sensations are only an association, the result of an emotional experience, and not the emotions themselves!* Equally, when you feel other sensations like "hungry, hot, cold, chilled, tired, fatigued, relaxed or sexually aroused," you're not feeling emotions either. You're feeling normal body sensations.

Feeling

Emotion

Moreover, when you have not learned to differentiate between normal body sensations and the impact that emotions have on your body, you'll tend to act on these body sensations believing that they are genuine emotions. *They are not.*

Example #2: One such sensation is the body sensation of sexual arousal being confused with the emotion "love." You might choose to move forward in a relationship believing that you *feel* "love" when the reality is that you're acting on sexual impulse. If your partner has a different paradigm than you do, about what the emotion of love truly is, your partner might not be able or willing to provide compatible behavior in return.

Anytime someone has mistaken sensation for emotion, confusion has occurred. Why might you confuse body sensations with emotions? The usual root cause for this is that you never learned (until now) to distinguish between body sensations and emotions.

YOU ARE NOT ALONE IN THIS

Our society as a whole does not take the time to communicate effectively (have you tried to understand cell phone "text" messages?) and the problems get worse when talking about emotions. Most people use words that actually denote body sensations when they are trying to share how they "feel." Children growing up with this method of communication tend to assume a great deal and therefore arrive at incorrect conclusions. In this respect, they have a learned emotional disadvantage.

In truth, you don't "feel" an emotion at all; you feel the energy shift that occurs because of the emotions you have generated. That shift has an effect on your body. If you don't take the time to distinguish between the "feel" of that shift and the "reason" and "cause" for the shift, you may believe them to be the same. You may even believe that the feeling *was* the emotion.

To compound the error of this false understanding, you may use "fuzzy" ways to communicate this, and that only confuses the

11

matter further. This kind of error comes about understandably. Like most people do, (think about cell phone "texting") you may abbreviate or "truncate" your expressions and say that you "feel" an emotion. Almost everyone does this in one way or another. Here's the truth though. You only "feel the effect" of the emotion, not the emotion itself. *To improve your emotional awareness you must differentiate sensations from emotions.*

Example #3: *"I feel courageous" actually means: I sense the shift in my body energy due to the effects of the emotion "courage" that I've generated by my thoughts.*

As you can see, *it is far easier and faster to say the shorter phrase* and assume that others know what you mean and will fill in the blanks. Trouble can occur though when neither you nor your listener realizes that there are blanks that need filling in.

As you read further, you might notice that I continue this "shortening" trend at specific points within this book. I hope that you'll be observant and notice when this occurs.

Noticing and appropriately using abbreviated emotional statements are important skills for improving your emotional awareness. Don't be fooled though into thinking that the abbreviated statement is truly accurate!

Exploration Opportunity:

1. Create a list of emotions you experience often.

2. Describe your sensations for each one for them.

2. There are No Buttons

Have you ever been with someone who pushes your buttons?

Did you notice that they know just what to say or do to set you off? Would it be fair to say that they really upset you at times?

Well, there's some news that you'll have to determine to be "good" or "bad" for you. *Brace yourself!*

YOU ARE THE SOLE CONTROLLER OF YOUR EMOTIONS

There are no buttons – they're imaginary and they reside in your head! This means that no one else makes you "feel" the way that you do. *This is regardless of the fact that thousands of song lyrics, books and constant dialog tell you otherwise.*

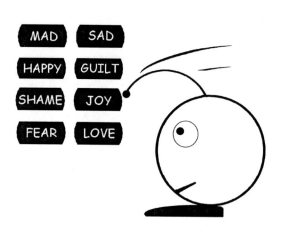

What most people view as "buttons" are really *habits*. These habits are reactions to the environment *that you don't think about* when you act them out. You're most likely to use the "button defense" when you get upset over things you do habitually in reaction to other people's behavior. The intention of this defense is to place *blame for your reactive behavior* on the other person *rather than the person who is truly responsible for* it – **you!**

More problems occur for you when accused "button" pushers play along with your view. When others are more aware of your habits than you are, especially those that require specific condition that "set you off," they may use your habits to your detriment. *All this occurs because you are not thinking about what you're doing!*

If you believe that people press your buttons and that people make you "feel" the way you do, *you believe an illusion.* Because of this belief, you'll also believe that others shouldn't hold you accountable for your actions. You may also abdicate your responsibility for what you experience emotionally and what you do as a result. Such choices play out this way. Of course, say and do all this and you'll be viewed as an "irresponsible and out of control" person by others whom know better.

You can change your habits. With a little bit of study and some strong commitment to know yourself, you can find out exactly what those imaginary buttons (reactive habits) are and learn how to both reprogram the useful ones and disconnect those that aren't.

Knowing what thoughts "trigger" your behavior helps you to choose effective behavior into the future.

Exploration Opportunity:

1. Create a list of all the people you know who have *"pushed your buttons"* at one time or another.
2. Create a list of the conditions each person on your list creates in your environment that brings you to the point of having *"your button pushed."*
3. For each time that your button is "pressed," write out – to the best of your ability – what you think it meant to you as *"your button is pressed."*

(Save your work. Come back to this after you read the "Commit to Explore & Improve" chapter.)

14

3. You Are in Control – Like It or Not

No one can make you "feel" angry, sad, upset, disappointed or happy. Conversely, you cannot "feel for" anyone else or cause others to generate any emotion; each of us "feels" for ourselves.

As was previously stated, there is no one else who can generate your emotions but you. To believe otherwise *is to believe an illusion.* No matter how much you might want to believe it and even point to examples in literature, movies and song, this fact isn't wrong. No memory you may use to justify your lack of control will change this fact. When you make effort to dismiss this fact, you create an unsafe condition for yourself and you base your choices on faulty information.

Example: *Someone does something that clearly violates Joe. The instant Joe perceives that violation he generates emotions like hurt, alarm and even confusion based on his relationship with that person. Joe perceives an instant later that he has the ability to protect himself from further violation and possibly change the situation so that he can reverse what has just occurred. He instantly generates anger.*

There is an important point to note though. The person who violated Joe didn't make him "feel" hurt, alarm or confusion and they did not make him "feel" angry. He generated these emotions on his own based on how he perceived his situation.

This is important to know because when you do experience an emotion, it's because you've generated it by thinking a specific way. You've chosen to believe and think specific things about your situation and as a result, you have created within you an

15

energy pattern perfectly tuned to what you think. *This same way of thinking applies for others!*

All the sensations that come about because of your emotions are a direct result of your thoughts. In this respect, you're totally responsible for those patterns and the impact of those patterns, as are others for theirs.

ANOTHER WAY OF SAYING THIS IS THAT YOU'RE RESPONSIBLE FOR EVERY EMOTION THAT YOU GENERATE – NO ONE ELSE IS

By default, just as you are responsible for the emotions you generate, everyone else is responsible for the emotions they generate – not you! We can all help what we think.

Exploration Opportunity:

1. Create a list of situations where you believed you were not responsible for how you felt and write out the emotions you experienced in those moments.

2. Write out what you were thinking just as those emotions occurred.

4. You Are NOT Your Emotions

*Know the difference between "Being" an emotion
and "Having" an emotion!*

A trap that many people fall into is acting as if they are their emotions. You'll hear this come out in conversation when emotions are in full swing.

Examples of this are as follows:

- *I am* so angry!
- *I am* sad to hear this.
- *I am* depressed about this loss.
- *I am* unbelievably happy to see you!
- *I am* fearful that I cannot do anything.
- *I am* frustrated that nothing works to fix this.
- *I am* grumpy when it rains.
- *I am* embarrassed to be here.

The common element is the telltale use of the words "I am" being used just before the emotion. Many people who use this wording and believe that what they say is true have gone from owning the emotion to having it "own" them. *This belief is an illusion* and an exceptionally strong one that people use to dismiss their personal accountability.

Do you want to gain control and ownership of the emotions you experience? If your answer is "yes," reword your expressions consciously to transform the "state of being" (I am…) claim into an expression of experience (I feel…).

Examples of this are as follows:

- *I feel* so angry!
- *I feel* sad to hear this.
- *I feel* depressed about this loss.
- *I feel* unbelievably happy to see you!
- *I feel* fearful that I cannot do anything.
- *I feel* frustrated that nothing works to fix this.
- *I feel* grumpy when it rains.
- *I feel* embarrassed to be here

As you can see, the change in wording moves the statement and the perception from "being" an emotion into "having" an emotion.

Notice too the <u>abbreviated form</u> of expressing emotions employed here as discussed in the "Feelings are not Emotions" chapter.

NOTE: *You can gain further ownership by stating "I have anger" or "I have sadness over this."*

These are important shifts in perception! They have you eventually possessing emotions instead of you believing they possess you!

Exploration Opportunity:

1. Create a list of sentences you've used or heard others use that have "I am," "I'm," "you are" or "you're" followed by an emotion.

2. Rewrite each of them so that they clearly state ownership.

3. Take another step and rewrite it to say that you "have" the emotion. **Examples:** *I have anger. I have sadness.*

5. Too Bad "Good" is Not an Emotion!

If "good" was an emotion, many people would know what they actually "feel."

However, they don't know how they "feel" if they use the word "good" to communicate emotions.

"Good" is not an emotion. Neither are "bad, awesome, great, fine, lousy, low, high" and any other word that denotes a judgment.

Using these words to describe emotions supports an illusion.

JUDGMENTS ARE NOT EMOTIONS

How can you tell whether a word you use for an emotion is a genuine emotion or merely a "judgment" type word *masquerading* as an emotion? Judgments masquerading as emotions only communicate a general value opinion of what you experience emotionally. A true  emotion gives you information about how you perceive your reality or what you are experiencing in your reality.

Example: The sentences, "I'm feeling great!" and "I'm feeling fine," don't convey any emotional information. *You base them both on value judgments about <u>what and how</u> you "feel."*

As you continue to gain awareness about emotions, you will encounter many words used by people to convey how they "feel." Don't be fooled though by words used which are not emotions.

Other Typical Judgment Words:

Astonishing	Junky	Special
Amazing	Kinky	Splendid
All right	Lame	Stupid
Acceptable	Lazy	Super
Agreeable	Miraculous	Terrific
Beyond belief	Nasty	Tired
Bodacious	Nice	Troubled
Cruddy	Okay	Tolerable
Crummy	Outstanding	Unusual
Decent	Perfect	Volatile
Extraordinary	Quick	Well
Fabulous	Raw	Wired
Fantastic	Reasonable	Wonderful
Grand	Remarkable	X-ed
Hairy	Rough	Yucky
Incredible	Satisfactory	Zany

Exploration Opportunity:

1. Create a list of words you normally use in response to the following question: "How do you feel?" *

2. Review these words and ask yourself whether they are emotions or judgments.

* **For future reference:** *"With my fingers!" is not an appropriate response for this question!*

6. Emotional Pluses & Minuses

*There are no such things as positive or negative (or good or bad or
right or wrong or toxic) emotions. Even though this is true, people
still tend to judge and then to call them this anyway! To believe
that emotions are positive or negative is to believe in an illusion.
Much like the judgments we may place on what we "experience"
emotionally are not the emotions themselves, labeling any emotion
as "positive" or "negative" is a judgment on the value of the
"emotion" experienced.*

Some people tend to judge and then label emotions that please or
displease them. This may be a way of simplifying talk about the
experienced emotions – sort of like a "short hand" way of
referencing them. Both "habits," labeling and simplifying, miss
much of what is truly occurring because these habits don't tell the
whole story. These habits may also give false assurances that what
a person judges and labels is "known" or understood. *This is an
illusion too.* Judging and labeling is only the *beginning* of
understanding,
not the end.

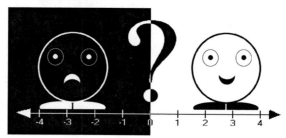

Further troubles
arise when we
think in dualistic
ways. Along
with this thinking
come value judgments that cause us unnecessary strife when we
experience healthy emotions and believe we are wrong in doing so.
If you think this way also, you might try to fight emotions that
arise as a normal and healthy result of living life. Doing so may
actually cause you to try to suppress your emotions. This only
causes further unnecessary strife and robs you of the rich
experience life has to offer you.

If you are one such person, be assured of the following:

EMOTIONS ARE NOT "POSITIVE OR NEGATIVE" IN ANY WAY

They are neutral. However, *how you choose to view them and act on them* can cause desired or undesired outcomes, which you may "label" as positive or negative.

Example #1: *Anger is an emotion that calls a person to take action to protect and/or cause change.* If you believe that anger is only a negative emotion, think back to a time about 2000 years ago. Records show an incredibly famous person in Western history overturned the tables of moneychangers who were occupying and disrespecting His Father's house. His **love** drove His action but the emotion He expressed was **anger**.

If you outlaw the emotion, "anger" because you judge that it can only be a negative emotion, then no responses to *calls to action to protect and cause change* will occur. As a result, no changes or protections that need to occur – for the good of a person's life or society as a whole – will occur. Households and organizations which want to maintain the status quo are much more inclined to discourage efforts to express anger because this edict allows them to continue on their chosen path unchecked and unchanged.

Example #2: *Fear is an emotion generated when a person perceives danger.* If you want to believe that fear is only a negative emotion, then ask yourself the following question: *Why would fear be one of the most successful emotions for making you aware that danger is present and for letting you know that you may need to take action to protect yourself from that danger?*

Example #3: *Guilt is an emotion that tells people that they perceive they have done wrong.* If you want to believe that guilt is only a negative emotion, then you choose to believe that it is a negative thing to know when you have done wrong. You have associated the wrongdoing with the emotion that tells you directly that you have not taken an honorable action. *Isn't it important to know how you view what you do, especially when you consider your action wrong by your moral code?*

Example #4 – *People usually perceive love and kindness as "positive" emotion, yet some people actually shy away from these emotions due to negative experiences and costs related to them.*

 Once again, the emotions themselves are not positive, negative, right, wrong, good or bad. Even claims that some emotions are "toxic" are misleading. Emotions in and of themselves are neutral. *It is how you perceive, judge and react to their messages that create the positive or negative view you hold about them.*

In other words, what you do with the messages your emotions present to you *will either enrich your life or make it toxic.* Your emotions aren't the problem, though your responses to them may be. Every emotion has importance.

IT IS CRITICAL TO YOUR LIFE CHOICES THAT YOU CLEARLY KNOW WHAT YOU TELL YOURSELF!

This becomes more evident as your emotional awareness improves.

Emotions are there to help you think about what you tell yourself. Thinking clearly and accurately improves your life choices and your life results.

Exploration Opportunity:

1. Create your own list of regularly experienced emotions.
2. Label them positive or negative as you might have prior to reading this chapter.
3. Examine each and ask yourself how you might experience them differently so that you experience them neutrally.

7. Emotional Reason, Logic & Rationale

An illogical & irrational belief held by some people is that emotions are illogical and irrational.

To belief that emotions are illogical and irrational *is to believe an illusion.* People who cannot deal with either the effects of emotions or the messages that emotions communicate are the one's most likely to hold this belief as true though. They believe that it is easier to dismiss emotions this way than to deal with the messages emotions present.

HERE'S THE TRUTH

Emotions are a *consequence –* an *outcome –* of thought. They are not the thought; *they are a symptom of the thought!* Emotions are not logical,

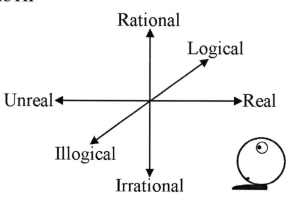

illogical, rational or irrational at all. The *thinking* that produces them may be any one (or more) of these things though.

Example: *Jo's partner is driving erratically. She tells him she's afraid and asks him if he took any drugs that could cause this behavior. He sips his beer then snaps indignantly "Absolutely not! You're being emotional again. Your irrational fear makes you think I did." Jo believes what he says. She had learned and accepted as true, in her alcoholic centered family, the false concept that alcohol is not a drug. Therefore, she dismissed the true message – **danger!***

24

LET'S REPLAY THIS

Jo faces a dangerous situation. She doesn't have time to confirm it or respond to it other than to realize that what is before her is indeed dangerous. Jo experiences fear to the degree that she believes that danger will affect her. Her thoughts of danger generate fear. <u>Jo looks at her options and chooses to take herself away from the danger</u>. She doesn't dismiss the message – danger.

It's irrational and illogical to classify fear as irrational or illogical when what is before you is indeed dangerous and your thoughts support it logically and rationally.

DO YOU WANT TO KNOW IF YOUR EMOTIONS ARE REAL OR REASONABLE?

The next time you have a very strong emotion affecting your body, try to do two things. Convince yourself in that moment 1) that the emotion you generate isn't real or 2) that it is not reasonable that you generate an emotion that makes effort to help you.

You'll find it very difficult to do since in the moment, the reality and reasonableness of your emotions will not be in question.

Exploration Opportunity:

1. Create a list of people you know who have dismissed your emotions and another list of the emotions you yourself have most often dismissed.

2. Examine the methods they (and you) used to dismiss them.

3. For every emotion, write out how you perceived the situation before you.

4. How supportive was each emotion to what you were thinking at those moments?

8. Emotions Are Not a Problem!

Believing that emotions <u>are a problem</u> causes <u>further difficulties</u>.

Emotions are merely symptoms of your thinking; hence, you can't "problem solve" them. *Focusing any effort in doing so will only frustrate you.* When you focus on the symptoms of a problem instead of on the causes, you might end up trying to mask or dismiss your emotions as the actual problem. They are not. Your thinking, especially your attitudes and beliefs, is where the problem resides. Once you're aware of this you'll more easily recognize that your emotions serve as messengers that will help you find the solution to the problem. *Killing the messenger doesn't kill the message!* However, doing so may only aggravate the problem since *you have focused on the symptom while leaving the cause of the problem unchecked.*

Example: *Jo receives honors that rightfully should go to Tara. But, Tara mistakenly believes that it's wrong for her to experience any **jealousy** so she decides to stop all feelings related to **jealousy** when they come up. She tries to "kill the emotion" rather than "deal with the true problem" – **someone else receiving honors that rightfully should be hers**. Tara's decision cascades to hurt & resentment aggravating relationships with others and her "self."*

Emotions are present for a reason. Validate that reason. Emotions can escalate into something bigger. Address the problem directly. Don't dismiss the emotion that tells you a problem exists. *Don't kill the messenger!*

Exploration Opportunity:

1. Describe a time when you believed emotions were a problem and why.
2. Describe the actual messages you believe those "problem" emotions were conveying.

9. Emotions Are Healthy!

Surviving & thriving depend on emotions.

If you ...

- *think you shouldn't have certain emotions*
- *take time and effort to fight having an emotion*
- *wish that you didn't have certain emotions*

...chances are you struggle because of previous training that preconditioned you to respond this way.

HEALTHY PEOPLE EXPERIENCE A WIDE RANGE OF EMOTIONS <u>ALL THE TIME</u>

Emotions are vital to grasping and dealing with your reality effectively. This makes them important aspects of your human makeup. *To believe that emotions are unhealthy or not normal is a dangerous illusion.*

Without emotions, you're less likely to thrive and your survival is at risk. *Emotions tell you what you perceive. It's better to examine your perception than your emotions. When everything is working, you experience emotions – and that's healthy!*

Exploration Opportunity:

1. What emotions do you tell yourself you shouldn't experience?"

2. Why are you telling yourself this?

3. What are those emotions telling you?

10. Emotional Wimp Factors

To openly "feel" and express emotions empowers you. How you do that in whatever culture you live depends on the cultural norms you wish to honor.

It's unfortunate that our mainstream Western society has such strong and counterproductive stereotypical views about having and expressing emotions. Too many people have preconceived notions as to what emotions are, what they do and what type of person expresses them. Collectively, this forms exceptionally strong cultural norms that are difficult to change.

Currently, if a male in power expressed sincere emotions in public, he's considered "in touch" with the more important things in life. Should a female in the same position do similar, she's viewed as "an emotional woman." **Right or wrong, you'll most likely not change this view for others.** You can though change the awareness and expression of your own views, enough to make a positive difference for yourself and those you care for most.

Example: *Jack cherishes a very old felt vinyl record cleaner he had from his days as a disc jockey. One day, his six-year-old son found it and used it as dry-marker erasure. Later that day Jack finds it all marked up on the floor. Jack realizes his son used it without asking him if it was okay. This is something that Jack has talked with his son about on numerous occasions. Anger occurs for Jack but he has trained himself to recognize his anger. His sadness & hurt over this discovery clearly shows on his face and in his body language.*

His young son sees this and asks his dad what's wrong. Jack expresses how hurt he feels about loosing something important to him that has been with him so long. His son realizes that he made a series of choices that harmed his dad. He sees the impact on his dad. Jack's son approaches his dad and hugs him. He apologizes and asks if he can fix it. Jack accepts his son's apology and works with his son to repair the damage.

This situation could have easily played out explosively. Far too many people would openly express anger in similar situations rather than focusing on what is truly at issue and responding accordingly.

Your strength lays not in repressing emotions but choosing the most <u>appropriate</u> way to express them within the context of any given situation.

Exploration Opportunity:

1. What emotions do you believe only wimps express?

2. What emotions are you less likely to express because you believe it would show weakness?

3. Why do you think this?

11. Emotion Sensitivity is Cyclic

Any chemical shifts – no matter how "normal" – create corresponding shifts in body sensitivity. This includes feeling emotional effects on your body.

Shifting cyclic hormone levels are one such influence. Humans have daily, weekly, monthly* and annual hormonal cycles. Cycles strongly depend on a person's *genetic makeup, age, diet, sleeping patterns and daily activities.*

Male or female, shifts in your body's chemical nature affect your thoughts. Once any shift occurs, it takes time to get used to those changes. Increased sensitivity usually occurs during this time. *Shifts can amplify any subtle changes that you would normally ignore. This can actually work to your advantage since increased sensitivity to shifts actually improves your awareness!*

Counter to this, other natural/pharmaceutical chemicals can override increased sensitivity due to hormonal shifts. (**Example:** *Endorphins can actually dull your awareness!*)

...

Note: Outside influences also affect overall sensitivity and hence mood. Changes in climate, daylight (seasonal and cloud cover), humidity, odors (including pheromones), medication and artificial lighting all have their effects. Each sets up changes that affect your overall sensitivity.

Exploration Opportunity:

1. Identify your personal key sensitivity indicators.
2. Use them to track your emotional sensitivity.
3. Discover your own sensitivity cycles.

* *Females typically 29-days; males typically 30-45 days; Adolescents typically 14 to 16 days*

12. Emotions Are Not Energy!

"What?" you might say. How can this be?

You might follow with "All my life I've been taught that emotions are energies and now you tell me that this is wrong!?" If you are thinking this, it's understandable and you are not alone. *Many of us learned to focus on the <u>symptoms of our emotions</u> instead of the <u>actual emotions themselves</u>.* This makes it exceptionally difficult to understand and accept a new paradigm.

When you focus on the symptoms alone, you might be tempted to *believe the illusion* that the energy you connect with during an emotional occurrence is the actual emotion itself. While this energy-emotion connection distracts you, it's easy to forget that this energy is already in your body; it's already part of your make up. Whether emotional patterns are present in that energy or not, that energy still exists within your body.

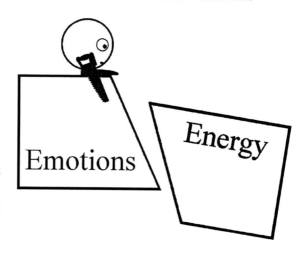

So what makes emotions different from the normal day-to-day energy that is already within your body? One must draw a distinction between the energy that is already present and when emotions manifest upon that energy to understand the difference.

The chapters that follow should clarify this distinction.

HERE IS A THOUGHT TO PONDER

In defending the belief that emotions are energy, you might argue that thoughts are energy and since thoughts generate emotions, emotions are energy too.

IT IS TIME FOR ANOTHER PARADIGM SHIFT

This is an illusion too. Thoughts are not energy. *Thoughts are* <u>patterns</u> *in and of energy; they are not the energy itself.*

*Transform your pattern of thought
and you will
transform your pattern of energy.*

Exploration Opportunity:

1. What emotions are you most likely to become aware of when they occur?

2. At what point did you actually sense that each emotion was present?

3. What body sensations were you feeling in those moments?

4. How would you describe the shift in energy driving these sensations?

II. Get Clear – Clarity!

You <u>see</u> the picture
only when your receiver
is properly tuned!

***

Clarity is the consciously lucid ability
to recognize the situation you have before you.
Your clarity may be so sharp that you already know
the situation's "foundations and possible outcomes.*"

* Also known as "alphas and omegas"

A. Then What Are Emotions?

*Emotions are patterns in your energies,
generated by your human body,
shaped by your thoughts and
supported by your mind's perceptions.*

In an extremely practical and simplistic way, emotions are the *shape of your body energies; your thoughts shape them.* You both generate and shape them, based on how you perceive your reality and how you support your thoughts.

Your thoughts automatically "shape" the energy that your body normally generates into a supporting pattern of energy that perfectly tunes to what you perceive. You identify the pattern of that energy as an "emotion."

EACH EMOTIONAL PATTERN YOU GENERATE IS UNIQUE IN ITS SPECIFIC QUALITY AND IS DISTINCT FROM OTHER EMOTIONAL PATTERNS.

This uniqueness lets you know that you have "internal pattern specific" support for what you perceive. Each also provides direct internal feedback on what you perceive.

There is a caveat though. You have a responsibility to verify that what you perceive is indeed valid for any given situation.

Emotions help you do this!

1. What Energy Patterns!?

Emotions are not energies; emotions are the <u>patterns of those</u> <u>energies</u>. Knowing this helps you focus on those patterns a lot quicker and more effectively.

Let's illustrate this with a simple "find the word in the puzzle" game.

At first glance, the puzzle on this page shows a mixed bunch of letters that for the most part show no overt pattern to them. As you review it, you might pick out one or two words that look familiar to you. You can do this because the letters form a pattern that you recognize as a word.

```
n o i s u f n o c t
o s y r o h u u h t
i u a v u o i o m s
t r e r n k p n n b
a p t r c e o b p r
r r a o e i m m i r
t i h m r a l a n s
s s e n i p p a h u
u e j r s s a d n s
r l o v e g u i l t
f f y d d a s d n h
```

Are all the letters spelling words? The answer is clearly "no."

Words have distinct patterns that have to occur in a specific way before you recognize each of them as words. If those patterns aren't present and correctly represented, you dismiss the letters before you as nonsense. When the pattern is correct, you "see" the word. The letters aren't the word though and no matter how many letters may make up a word, the letters are still not the word.

ENERGY IS TO EMOTIONS AS LETTERS ARE TO WORDS

No matter how much or how little energy is present, the energy will never "be" the emotion just like no matter how many letters are present, they – the letters – will never "be" the word. *Emotions shape your energy much like letters shape words.* Only when the pattern of that energy has a specific shape can you recognize the emotion that caused that shape.

35

Inspect the list of words found within the "Exploration Opportunity" section of this page. You may notice that you have letters in a specific pattern that you should recognize to be words denoting emotions. Each of these words would not be the same if you arrange the letters differently. Likewise, none would be the same if some of the letters were missing. This includes situations where you may recognize them in their truncated form – in context.

The same thing applies with emotion. The pattern must be complete and specific for an emotion to "be." Is it any wonder why most people confuse the energy with the emotion? They do not think about the pattern of that energy and only focus on the energy itself. In doing so, they miss out on what the emotion has to offer.

It is quite clear that energy and emotions go hand in hand – just like letters and words – but what may not be clear is that the pattern of that energy is what makes it an emotion, just like the pattern of letters make a word.

Of course, by now you might have guessed that just as *words* have specific and general meanings, *so do emotions!*

Exploration Opportunity:

1. Have some fun! Can you find within the "Word Search" above all the following listed emotions? *Alarm, Despair, Desire, Sad, Happiness, Shock, Envy, Hurt, Numb, Frustration, Hate, Joy, Pain*

2. Which Comes First?

Do thoughts cause your emotions? Do emotions cause your thoughts? The answers to both questions are "yes."

If this seems to be a bit too simple and a bit "fuzzy," let me ask a different question. What starts the cycle of "thought-emotion" events? This question is much easier to answer and gives a much clearer picture. The answer is that "thoughts" start the "thought-emotion" cycle of events, even if it may appear otherwise.

LET'S CLARIFY THIS

You, as a healthy human being, start with a thought, conscious or otherwise. Your thought generates an emotion. You think about that emotion at some level, consciously, subconsciously or even unconsciously. Either your thought re-enforces that emotion or you generate another emotion instead.

Example #1: *Bob thinks about something that is funny. He generates an emotion that is like joy or delight. At some level, he senses how delighted & amused he feels. Bob finds delectation in this and more delight and more joy type emotions occur. This may continue until he exhausts himself to the point that discomfort occurs.*

Example #2: *Dee thinks she's in a dangerous situation. She generates the emotion fear. If she thinks it's dangerous to feel fear, she increases the intensity of that fear; she may even generate panic. If she thinks she should face the fear and is willing to do so, she generates courage.*

THOUGHT STILL COMES FIRST THOUGH

All this may occur in a split second and without *conscious* thought! When this cycle occurs without conscious thought, you "react" out of habit rather than "respond" thoughtfully. Automatic behavior does not require you to think about what you normally habitually do. To change outcome, you must change behavior. To change behavior, you must first think about what you are doing. These are important connections since improving your Emotional Awareness requires you to respond and not react!

Responses require conscious thought; reactions don't.

Exploration Opportunity:

1. What dominant emotions fill your life?

2. What do you think about these emotions?

3. What thoughts usually precede each of these emotions?

4. What actions do you usually take when each of these emotions occur?

5. What connection do you make between your dominant thoughts, emotions and actions?

3. Why Emotions?

Why not!? Emotions have four supportive purposes and each of these is supportive of your life!

TUNE

The first purpose of emotions is <u>to tune perfectly your body's energy</u> to assist you in dealing with the reality you perceive before you.

No matter what you perceive, an emotion perfectly tunes your body energy to help you deal with that perception. This is automatic and without a doubt a good thing most of the time since pondering too long on things that require quick action may actually cause you harm.

Example: *Chip perceives danger. His emotion shifts his body energy pattern to deal with what he perceives. In so doing, he experiences an energy pattern supporting fear.*

VALIDATE

The second purpose of emotions is <u>to let you know what you perceive</u> in the moment.

When you know the messages that any specific emotion communicates to you, you're better able to judge what you perceive before you and make choices accordingly.

Example: *Amy knows that emotions tell her how she perceives her reality. Amy experiences fear and recognizes the feel of the emotion "fear" transforming the energy in her body. She knows she perceives danger before her. Amy takes actions to minimize the danger.*

IMPRINT

> *The third purpose is <u>to strengthen and temper the relevance of specific patterns in your memory and your typical responses</u> to these patterns.*

As life unfolds, specific situational patterns become more or less relevant. Typically, the more emotionally intense a pattern, the more intense the pattern's memories and your future responses; less emotional intensity brings less intense pattern memories and responses. When you encounter those patterns again, your pattern recognition and memory recall usually work to your benefit. They bring to your awareness, at some level, the significance of what is before you and create automatic and equally significant typical responses toward that pattern.

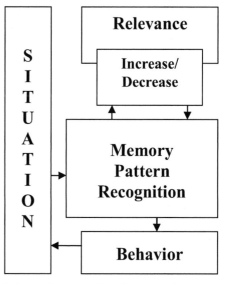

Example #1: *Emma is standing on the side of a busy street she is about to cross. Her gut tells her the situation before her is dangerous. She knows the feeling; she has had it before. Before she knows consciously what she is doing, she steps back from where she is standing. A car – which she was only subconsciously aware of – sweeps across the very spot she was standing only seconds before. The intensity of her traffic experiences created a recognizable pattern for Emma at some level to create an appropriate automatic behavior to the situation before her. Emma suffers no ill affects from the experience. She counts her blessings that her intuition and response were able to prevent a serious situation.*

Unfortunately, sometimes the intensity of an experience or a series of experiences (real or imagined) are so overwhelming that the pattern recognition and automatic responses become inappropriate. It doesn't matter if this occurs because of a single traumatic event or through conscious or unconscious self-programming. The eventual outcome is a real and serious effect.

Example #2: *Kay and her sister drive on a mountain road with steep embankments. Kay misses a sharp turn, her car flies off the road and comes to rest on top of a telephone pole. They're a bit bruised and emotionally shocked but are otherwise physically unharmed. A local police officer comes upon the scene and Kay asks him to call their mom, Jen. He contacts Jen, tells her that her children are okay, and requests that she come to the scene.*

When Jen arrives, she views the scene and is immediately aware of what could have occurred. She sees that the pole went through the car's bottom just behind the front seats and was stopped by the inside roof of the car. Jen realizes that her children are very fortunate. They could have suffered any number of injuries or possible deaths.

The patterns of the event were extremely intense for Jen. She continues to obsess for some time afterward about the different possibilities that could have occurred to her children. Although the original event didn't occur to Jen, her imagination brings forth intense emotions and body responses imprint due to each imagined possibility.

As Jen encounters situations involving driving and height, the patterns bring forth memories and body responses increasingly more intense with each encounter. Jen's fear eventually immobilizes her with every instance she encounters involving driving and heights.

COMMUNICATE

The fourth purpose of emotions is <u>to communicate with others</u> what you perceive in the moment and for you to do the same in kind.

Your survival may depend upon others knowing your situation and visa versa. When people know what others experience, they're better able to communicate and take appropriate social actions.

Example: *Fran's body language shows fear. Others approaching her keep their distance until Fran outwardly shows she's more secure to their advances. Fran recognizes them as friends. She shows calm and joy. They approach her.*

Exploration Opportunity:

1. What other purposes do you notice emotions have in life?

2. How well are you able to sense your emotion tuning your body's energy? What are the most obvious signs?

3. How well are you able to identify the emotion you generate? What are the most prominent perceptions?

4. Which of your behaviors are clearly due to imprinting? Are they life nurturing or do they deplete your energy?

5. How well are you able to notice the emotions others are generating? How well can those you know best read your emotions?

6. If you are a person of faith or spiritual by nature, how well do you communicate with your "Higher Power?" What do you notice most being communicated to you?

4. Who Drives Emotions?

Without a doubt, you do.

As shared in an earlier chapter, your "VIPE" (Values, Intentions, Perception and Experiences) influence your thoughts. Your thoughts also influence your VIPE in return. Emotions are a symptom of all this and *it's all you!*

You might consider two aspects when you want to know more about the driver though.

THE FIRST ASPECT IS THE <u>CHOICE</u> OF EACH EMOTION

As shared before, emotions are symptoms of thought. This means thoughts create emotions automatically. In this sense, your choice of emotion doesn't occur directly. The only control you have over choice is the control you have over your thoughts.

As scary as this might seem for some people, this is for an important reason and it makes valuable sense. If you had to develop consciously all that's involved with emotions, you would likely not develop them at all. This would leave you vulnerable and potentially prevent your survival.

Let's break down the first aspect – *your choice of emotion.* As shared before, emotions are a result of thoughts. To choose your emotion, you must choose your thoughts. As you might already realize, controlling your thoughts is not an easy task. It's next to impossible at times. When it can be done, some control occurs indirectly with improved awareness. That's the basis of this book.

Improve your emotional awareness and improve your ability to control your emotions.

Let's look at what's involved.

Your mental component (thought) is comprised of four subcomponents – *values, intents, perceptions and experiences.* They all interconnect.

Let's take a closer look at these sub-components:

- **Values** – *patterns you have deemed worthy or unworthy*
- **Intentions** – *patterns that you want most or least*
- **Perceptions** – *patterns in which you see or don't see your world*
- **Experiences** – *habitual patterns formed as a result of your memories and history*

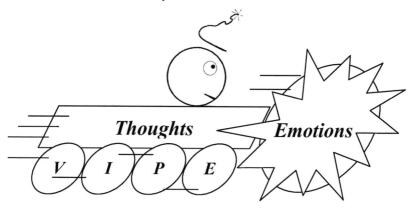

Your VIPE come together to form your thoughts. You have no control over how they come together. *You only have control over your choice of values, intentions and experiences along with how you choose to perceive them in relation to what is before you.* This means you can influence your pattern of thoughts by consciously influencing your VIPE! They are *your thought's foundation.*

As your thoughts form, you automatically generate specific patterns you recognize as emotions. In other words, your collective thoughts about what is before you determine your emotions.

If you want to know more about what influences *your* emotions, you must start with your thoughts. Restating the same list above but more personally, you have the following list to consider:

- **Your Values** – The standard ideals you hold dear as worthy, beneficial, useful or otherwise in making your choices. They include the people, places or things you believe to be of importance, relevance, significance or consequence to your life.
- **Your Intentions** – The purposes, aims, goals, targets, objectives, and plans you seek to achieve.
- **Your Perceptions** – The biasing filters you connect with and view you world though.
- **Your Experiences** – Your collective memories, knowledge, understanding, biases and skills developed over your lifetime.

Each of these affects the other and the ultimate result of this interconnection is an emotion that perfectly matches what you perceive. *If there is any truth behind the saying "perception is reality," then you can thank your perception for creating your emotional reality.*

HOW YOU THINK AND WHAT YOU THINK CREATES YOUR WORLD

Example: *Sue is about to give a presentation for a group of 30 people. She previously agreed to do this for a 50-50 split of the income generated. The group's supporting staff approaches her and ask if the 50-50 split is okay. Sue thought that this was all predetermined yet the question is before her. She values consistency. She expresses confusion over the fee arrangement. The staff members misread her confusion and think that she is* *indicating the fee might not be enough. They increase the offer to a 60-40 split.*

Although Sue <u>values</u> more money, she also <u>values</u> her integrity; couple this with <u>experiences</u> where she didn't honor her word and her <u>intention</u> to continue doing business with integrity into the future. She <u>perceives</u> their fear and her own as well. Sue quickly says, "Thanks but I already agreed to a 50-50 split and this is sufficient."

She sees the immediate relief on their faces and feels her body relax. Sue honors her values and intentions. What she perceived was accurate. Her <u>experiences</u> were well utilized. Sue's awareness paid off!

Every sub-component comes into play as you navigate through life.

You generate or "*drive*" emotions by what you think.

Exploration Opportunity:

1. What are five values you hold highest above all others?

2. What are five intentions for which you continuously strive?

3. What five perceptions do you tend to rely on no matter what?

4. What five experiences to you tend to recall most often when dealing with situations in your life?

5. How About Intensity?

The __second aspect__ that drives emotions is the relative intensity of each emotion created.

This is your emotional "power controller." It determines the amplitude or power of your emotion for any given situation. This aspect you do have control over and your control depends both on your emotional awareness and your internal responses to your awareness.

LET'S LOOK AT HOW THIS WORKS

Your emotional intensity is a direct function of how the four sub-components of your thinking influence each other. They collectively work to produce a level of intensity that assists you in dealing with what is before you.

1. Your overall *emotional awareness* lets you know many things.
   - **Who** generates the emotion
   - **Why** it was generated
   - **What** it communicates
   - **When** and **where** an emotion occurs *(situation)*
   - **How** it affects you and others *(including how soon and how long that affect occurs)*

2. Your *skills* and *habits* determine your *treatment* of this information.
   - Your ability to **evaluate** and **appraise** what is before you and *how you apply* this ability
   - Your ability to discern its **relevance, urgency** and **importance** to you *as it relates* to you
   - Your view toward *how it serves or impacts* your **interests** and **concerns** and the *length of time it serves you*

3. Your *experience* and *habitual manner* determine how successful you generate an *appropriate* level of intensity.

- Your ability to **recall** and **apply** *experience* and *knowledge* will **regulate** and **temper** your **internal** and **external** *behavior*

In other words, you're more likely to generate emotional intensity **appropriate** to the situation before you when you…

- know what your emotion tells you
- evaluate your emotion's relevance clearly
- know how it serves your interests
- know how to respond to it effectively

Example: *Ann's supervisor approaches her. She asks if Ann has any anxiety about her new job. Ann tells her no and asks her why. She tells Ann that one of her coworkers told the supervisor's assistant that Ann had anxiety about her job. She said she was concerned and thought she might be able to help.*

Ann realizes immediately that she is concerned about how her supervisor views her honesty. Ann has concern that her response reflects poorly on her coworker. Ann knows that her coworker already has some opposition with the supervisor's assistant. Ann's anxiety intensifies. She leaves work with her head spinning in confusion and further anxiety. Ann finds herself driving home nervously laughing at the irony of the situation.

Upon arriving home Ann's husband notices her overall agitation. He says that she appears to be intensely anxious and asks what occurred. Ann lets him know about her work conversation. He waits until she's finished and then reminds her that she was wrongly instructed as to where and when the orientation meeting was that first day. He adds that Ann didn't like arriving late and that she arrived late to the meeting. He says he remembers that she let her coworker know of her anxiety about being late. He says he sure can understand why Ann would be so anxious about this situation.

Upon hearing her husband's words, Ann realizes how it all fits together. Her anxiety is gone. Ann experiences relief. Her coworker was accurate in what she said about Ann having anxiety. Ann knows what to do.

The next day Ann lets her supervisor know that there was indeed an anxious moment due to the miscommunications that took place over the meeting time and location. It was not about the job itself.

Exploration Opportunity:

1. What do you see contributing to your thoughts?

2. What might you add to the aspects and sub-components in the lists above?

3. How do you see all these components contributing to what you think?

4. Explore words that you might use to describe low intensity. *Here are a few examples: Impassive, Stoic, Phlegmatic, Apathetic, Stolid*

5. Explore words that you might use to describe high intensity. *Here are a few examples: Impassioned, Passionate, Ardent, Fervent, Fervid, Perfervid*

6. *Retake the quiz on page 9 and compare any changes to your responses to it. What changed for you?*

6. Where's the Regulation?

Many ways to regulate emotions exist. Some have their "pros and cons." What works best varies from person to person and from one situation to the next.

This topic truly warrants another book to cover adequately. What you read here is a very brief overview with targeted points to assist you toward improving your emotional awareness. Should anything herein spark an interest, please explore this topic further after you complete this book.

What you have read so far is a quick and intense overview of how you generate and regulate your emotions. *This section is where you learn how to identify types of regulation that can work for you or against you.*

REGULATION

Feedback Loop

Regulation *creates a "feedback loop" that helps you deal with what is before you.* Feedback loops work best when your behavior directs you toward results that affirm your life.

Press to Motivate

Functional and Healthy Regulation of emotions occurs *when you respond effectively to the affects of the emotions you generate.* You know what the emotions tell you and take appropriate actions in response to them. Your actions acknowledge, accept and affirm those emotions so they serve their purposes. *Regulation occurs automatically by using the messages, tuned energies and created behavior to help direct emotions toward closure.* Closure occurs when the emotion's purposes are served. Once any emotion's purposes are served, there is no more need for you to generate that emotion – until similar situations occur again. *Life goes on, as it should.*

Dysfunctional and Unhealthy Regulation of emotions occurs *when you make effort – at some level – to dismiss, alter, deny, distract, divert, or mask emotions because of the unwelcome message or sensations those emotions bring forth.* In this case, once any emotion occurs that is unwelcome for any reason, your next intended actions sabotage the purposes emotions serve. Unfortunately, most people caught up in this sabotaging behavior don't do it consciously! *That's why it is so important to improve your awareness to avoid this.*

MOOD ALTERING

This sabotage is called, "**Mood Altering.**" It attacks either the very thoughts that generate unwelcome emotions or their effects – the sensations that occur due to emotions shifting your body's energy and chemistry. *Both attacks create multiple problems and further difficulties in life.*

Internal Problems: Your mind's thoughts tend to want validation and your body tends to want to take action based on the tuning of its energy. When neither occurs, a cascade of thoughts and body sensations re-enforcing the original emotion may be the result. This only aggravates the original situation and doesn't support the emotion's purposes. *The emotion's intensity may actually increase.*

External Problems: The situation before you requires attention and the message of your behavior is inconsistent with what the situation demands. When you don't respond appropriately, the situation before you remains unaddressed and the people surrounding you can't support you in a healthy nurturing way. This can aggravate the original situation and it doesn't support the emotion's purposes. *Life continues to get more difficult. Mood Altering to avoid dealing effectively with what is before you is truly counterproductive behavior.* This behavior tends to fall into three dominant categories.

The first category is <u>*process*</u> *related.* It works on your mind's ability to keep focused on what creates the emotion in question. Its intent is to distract your mind from thinking about what is before you. By creating different thinking patterns through focusing your attention off what was causing an undesired emotion, there is momentary relief from that emotion. When you engage in a process with a specific underlying intent to alter thoughts or body sensations attributed to undesired emotions, you have a *Process Related Mood-Altering Situation* (**PRMS**).

HERE ARE SOME PRMS EXAMPLES:

- <u>*Purposeful Distractions:*</u> *Preoccupations, Creative Avoidances, Time Wasting Socializing, Care-taking Others, Unhealthy Relationships & Codependent Behaviors*
- <u>*Compulsive:*</u> *Hobbies, Shopping, Reading, TV, Movies, Web Surfing, E-mail, Sleep & Meditation*
- <u>*Obsessing*</u> *in General: Cleaning, Preparing*
- <u>*Detailing*</u> *in Thinking, Writing and Conversation*
- *Reality* <u>*Denial*</u> *Systems of Thought*

The second category is <u>*substance*</u> *related.* It works on masking and altering your body sensations. When you take a substance with the specific intent to alter thoughts or body sensations attributed to undesired emotions, you have a *Substance Related Mood-Altering Situation* (**SRMS**).

HERE ARE SOME SRMS EXAMPLES:

- *Food, Caffeine, Alcohol, Smoking, Inhalants, and Drugs*

The last category is a combination of the first two. When you engage in activities with the specific intent to generate chemical changes within you body to alter/distort thoughts or body sensations attributed to undesired emotions, you have a *Process Induced-Substance-Related Mood-Altering Situation* (**PIMS**).

HERE ARE SOME PIMS EXAMPLES:

- *Adrenaline and Endorphin Producing Activities; Self-Induced Stress Creating Situations; Sex (with or sans partners); Gambling; Sports; Exercise; Work; Diet, Delays.*

All three previous category examples in and of themselves may not indicate *mood altering* involvement. They're presented here to let you know that each can be used to your detriment.

Habitual Mood-Altering Behaviors may be a form of counter-productive addiction, no matter how mild they may appear.

SOMETHING TO NOTE!

The "90 Second" Window: *Healthy bodies normalize chemicals created by emotion generation within about 90 seconds. Unresolved emotions and recycling thoughts drive emotional affects that continue beyond this point.*

Exploration Opportunity:

1. What behaviors do you use most to regulate your emotions? Create a list.

2. Which listed behaviors do you know you could improve toward more affirming actions?

3. Based on what you know, what efforts must you make to improve your regulation?

4. Create an action plan to implement what you know could be done to improve your results.

7. When is Mood Reality?

Unlike emotions, moods have a much longer shelf life. They can last a few minutes or an entire lifetime.

The root of the word "mood" originally meant "frame of mind," and it still holds that meaning to this day. Mood is "a condition, an aspect and a tendency" and hence dictates your "state of being." (*As you thinketh in your heart, so you are!"*) The persistence of any mood depends on a series of choices on your part.

Mood ascendancy **is** due to **a fixation of thoughts** that dominate your whole being. Those thoughts affect your body chemistry and color all that you view. Your energy levels and perception, and **hence your reality**, are greatly affected by your mood. The relationship is circular; your mood also affects your energy levels and your perception.

When specific moods are present, you know that either a specific emotion or group of emotions have taken root and have made themselves "at home." Since moods affect your choices, it is wise to be conscious of your mood and strive to make your choices only when you know that your mood supports your true goals.

Moods are cyclic in nature. Keeping track of your moods can help you to *reasonably* predict when to engage in activities that support richer life experiences and results. Be aware that this activity is extremely subjective. Devise your tracking chart *to include all elements that affect you personally.*

Exploration Opportunity:

1. Identify five primary moods that occur for you regularly.
2. When you are most likely to have these moods?
3. Explain why and who might be involved and *what can you do to maximize or minimize the impact of your moods?*

III. Get in Touch – Connect!

You'll <u>feel</u> the rhythm
And <u>hear</u> the words
only when your receiver
is properly engaged!

***

Connection occurs when you are fully engaged
with the reality of the situation before you.

Your connection depends
on how well you <u>grasp</u> the situation.

Emotions as Messengers

Imagine yourself to be a receiver. Every time you receive information, you generate a thought that brings forth an emotion that writes into your body energy a pattern that has an incredibly specific and unique <u>message</u>.

Knowing what these special and unique patterns are and what they *say gives you an advantage over people* whom never take the time

to explore their inner messages. There should be no doubt that the messages are inside each of us. All you have to do is reach within them within, get a firm grip and unroll them to look at the messages you receive.

Once you do, you might be pleasantly surprised to find what has been there all along!

Let's explore what some of these messages might be.

...

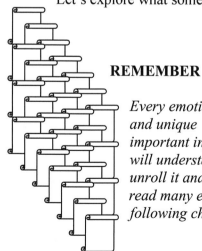

REMEMBER

Every emotion that you generate has a specific and unique "<u>rolled up</u>" message that tells you important information about your life. You will understand the message if you choose to unroll it and examine it for what it is. You'll read many examples of these messages in the following chapters.

A. Exploring Different Types of Messages

We assign meaning to words.
Why not do the same for emotions?

There are thousands of words which are used to convey emotional experiences. Many of them happen to fall into a handful of categories having to do with the following emotions:

- **Comfort** - *Like, Calm, Pleasure*
- **Value** - *Interest, Investment, Divestment*
- **Change** - *Anticipation, Danger, Loss*
- **Discomfort** - *Lack, Dislike, Provocation, Pain*
- **Complex** - *Mixed, Saturation, Social, Echo, Secondary, Ed*

Let's look at these categories now, see which emotions you might find in each category and what the message is that you might glean from each emotion. The lists that follow are in no way complete. Some of the emotions listed could fit into more than one category. *Once you have learned to recognize each pattern within yourself, you will be able to use what you learned to create your own lists or to refine those offered in this book as they apply to you.*

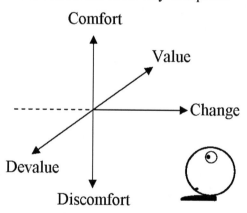

One final note to ponder: *The word "angel" comes from the Latin root "angelus," which means "messenger." So, in a very literal sense, emotions are in every way our "angels." This book helps you understand them more quickly, more easily and have less confusion.*

1. COMFORT – Calm, Pleasure, Like

Comfort Emotions relate to the empowering resources one can draw from. All of them follow this theme of empowering but with many variations.

Comfort – Meaning "with strength," this emotion occurs for those who know they *have support for dealing with whatever is before them.*

CALM EMOTIONS

Calm Emotions relate to calming effects on thoughts and the body.

Calm Emotions are **Comfort Emotions** which tell you that you're "okay" with what is before you. These emotions give you information about how you view your situation and why you're okay with it.

The emotions listed below are variations on the "calm" theme and have accompanying information that may help you have better understanding when that emotion occurs.

...

Serene – From a Latin root meaning "bright, clear," this emotion occurs for those *with sharp clarity on issues of interest.*

Peaceful – From the root word denoting "to fasten so as to achieve a stable condition," this emotion occurs for people who *achieve stability within.*

Secure – Originally, meaning, "care free," this emotion occurs for those *with sufficient safeguards or assurance.*

Tranquil – From a root word akin in meaning to "over, beyond + rest, quiet, calm," and used for the Moon's "Sea of Tranquility," this emotion occurs for people *free from disturbance or agitation.*

Confident – From the root meaning, "to place one's trust & faith," this emotion occurs for those who *believe all is well within what they are engaged.*

Acceptance – From the root meaning, "take to oneself" and as well as being the last stage of the grieving process, this emotion occurs for those who *favorably receive, embrace or approve of who or whatever is before them without reservation or stressful disturbance.*

Shame – Often inappropriately associated with *one's relative value or worth**, this emotion in actuality is the source of *true humility* and it occurs for people who both *recognize & live within their true limitations, values and abilities with ease and comfort.*

Exploration Opportunity:

1. How many other calm emotions can you find in the "Quiz Yourself" section of the appendix?

2. Which specific calm emotions are you most likely to experience?

3. What do you usually have going on around you when these emotions come up?

4. Describe the following emotions: Ease, Fulfillment, Complacent, Contentment, Placid, Sate, Sure

* *See* **Lack Emotions – Inadequate** *for what some people call* **"Toxic Shame"**

PLEASURE EMOTIONS

Pleasure Emotions relate to desired or "sought for" mental or physical states that gratify.

Pleasure Emotions are **Comfort Emotions** that tell you that gratification has occurred. These emotions give you information about how you perceive the gratification.

The emotions listed below are variations on the "pleasure" theme and have accompanying information that may help you have better understanding when that emotion occurs.

Delight – From the Latin root word meaning, "to entice from," this emotion occurs for those who are *greatly satisfied.*

Happy – From a root-word meaning, "by chance," and wished for by many, this emotion occurs for those who are *content and have a strong sense of well being.*

Merry – From a common root associated with the word "mirth" meaning "jolly" and alluded to three times in a common children's song (merrily,...), this emotion occurs for those *with high-spirits and lightheartedness.*

Joy – From a Latin root meaning, "rejoice," and found in the title (Jesu, Joy of Man's Desiring) of one of J. S. Bach's musical masterpieces, this emotion commonly occurs for those who *have a deeply moving experience of satisfaction and pleasure.*

Glad – Originally meaning "bright, shining" and used in polite conversation, this emotion commonly occurs for those who _experience mild gratitude and joy._

Cheerful – Originally, meaning, "face," this emotion occurs for those whose _joy and merriment tends to animate them both physically and verbally and who are likely to dispel gloom or worry._

Relief* – Literarily meaning "to rise again" or "to rise back" this emotion occurs for those who _are no longer "held down" mentally._

Exploration Opportunity:

1. How many other pleasure emotions can you find in the "Quiz Yourself" section of the appendix?

2. Which specific pleasure emotions are you most likely to experience?

3. What do you usually have going on around you when these emotions come up?

4. Describe the following emotions: Console, Jolly, Jovial, Delectation, Reminiscence, Contentment, Jocund, Satisfaction, Agog, Amusement, Blithe, Jubilation, Elation, Thrill, Gusto, Exultation

* _This is also a_ **Divestment Emotion**

LIKE EMOTIONS

Like Emotions relate to a partiality or preference for specific people, situations, places or things.

Like Emotions* are a category of **Comfort Emotions** that tell you that a bias toward or favoring for is occurring. These emotions give you information about how you perceive that bias and favoring.

The emotions listed below are variations on the "like" theme and have accompanying information that may help you have better understanding when that emotion occurs.

...

Affinity – From the Latin root meaning, "bordering on something," denoting a "relationship," this emotion occurs for those with *an attraction based on relationship or underlying connection.*

Like – Originally meaning, "pleasing," this emotion occurs for those who *have a bias toward whatever is the focus of their attention and who have pleasure in that focus.*

Fond – Originally meaning, "foolish" and whose modern meaning implies "great liking," this emotion occurs for those who *have an excessive, overindulgent or unreasonable bias or inclination toward what is the focus of their attention.*

Fancy – From the same root as "fantasy" meaning, "to show," this emotion occurs for those who *favor people, places or things suddenly, impulsively and unpredictably.*

Attraction – From the root-word originally meaning, "to pull something towards one," this emotion occurs for those *drawn or pulled toward whatever is the focus of their attention.*

Appeal – From a nautical term meaning, "to direct a ship toward a destination," this emotion occurs for those who are *directed toward whatever is the focus of their attention.*

Passion – From a root meaning, "to suffer, endure," this emotion occurs for those who are *demonstratively willing to endure or suffer due to an intense or extreme appeal.*

Exploration Opportunity:

1. How many more "like" emotions can you find in the "Quiz Yourself" section of the appendix?

2. Which specific like emotions are you most likely to experience?

3. What do you usually have going on around you when these emotions come up?

4. Describe the following emotions: Affection, Acceptance

* **Like Emotions** *also have some* **Value Emotion** *aspects to them. People tend to like what they value.*

2. VALUE – Interest, Investment, Divestment

Value Emotions relate to worth & importance.

Value Emotions tell you the significance to you of what is before you *(one person's trash is another person's treasure)*. Each variation on this emotional theme gives you further information about how you value whatever is before you.

The emotions listed below are variations on the "value" theme and have accompanying information that may help you have better understanding when that emotion occurs.

...

Pride – From the root word meaning, "value," this emotion occurs for those who *value whatever or whoever is before them.*

Appreciation – From an "investment term" meaning, "to increase in value," this emotion occurs for those who *sense additional value to them in whatever or whoever is before them.*

Admiration – Originally meaning, "to marvel," this emotion occurs *when people "highly approve and respect" whatever or whoever is before them.*

Gratitude – Originally meaning, "pleasing, thankful," this emotion occurs for those who *realize that the benefit they are enjoying has come from a specific source.*

Reverence – From a Latin root meaning, "to hold in awe or fear," this emotion occurs for those who *respectfully value who or what is before them, often with vigilant tenderness.*

Contempt – From the Latin root meaning, "scorn" and discouraged in legal courts, this emotion occurs for people who are *overtly disrespectful, disdainful or irreverent.*

Guilt* – From Middle English meaning, "delinquency," this emotion occurs for those who have *transgressed something they value.*

Arrogant – From the Latin compound root meaning, "to claim for oneself," this emotion occurs for people who *believe they have more value than they actually do (Proudly Contemptuous).*

Exploration Opportunity:

1. How many other value emotions can you find in the "Quiz Yourself" section of the appendix?

2. Which specific value emotions are you most likely to experience?

3. What do you usually have going on around you when these emotions come up?

4. Describe the following emotions: Respect, Honor, Adore, Esteem, Humility, Smug, Disgrace, Humiliation, Dishonor, Degradation

*   **NOTE:** *You can program yourself to generate guilt when you've truly done nothing wrong. Some people call this emotional response* **"Toxic Guilt***." This is the result of dysfunctional thinking and conflicting values. It can lead to needless pain, anxiety & adaptive behavior: i.e. low quality boundaries, perfectionism & attempting to control others.)*

INTEREST EMOTIONS

Interest Emotions are <u>value</u> based and show a degree of speculative importance to the person who so generates one or more of them.

Interest Emotions are **Value Emotions** which tell you that you have interest in what or who is before you. By refining your awareness of this emotion, you help yourself to more readily recognize specific emotions within this category and thereby give yourself more information about that interest.

The emotions listed below are variations on the "interest" theme and have accompanying information that may help you have better understanding when that emotion occurs.

...

Desire – Denoting "aspiration, or an inspired goal," this emotion occurs for those who *imagine and then seek a worthwhile goal.*

Want – Originally meaning, "lacking" and filled with firm resolve "to bring about," this emotion occurs for those *longing to obtain or achieve something they desire but do not need.*

Wonder – Filled with uncertainty and conjecture, this emotion occurs for those *drawn toward things of interest.*

Long – As in "to *long* for." Often referring to a "length of time or distance," this emotion occurs for those who *heart-fully desire something remote and not easily attainable.*

Yearn – Associated with physical discomfort, this emotion occurs for people who *desire something so much that they produce <u>discomfort</u> to their body.*

Envy* – Long thought to be a "green eyed monster," this emotion arises when people also *desire for themselves that which another person already possesses.* (*At times, this experience may include elements of* **Discontent** *and* **Resentment**.)

Jealous* – The motivation for many frictions between lovers, partners and friends, this emotion occurs when people *believe they rightfully own or deserve to own that which is possessed by or bestowed upon another.*

Covetous* – From a root word meaning, "desire" and closely related to "cupidity" this emotion occurs for those who *intensely desire what rightfully belongs to another.*

Greed – With near meaning with "covetous," this emotion occurs for those *with excessive, unrestrained and often indiscriminant desire.*

Lust** – From the Germanic root meaning, "desire," and found among the proscribed emotions that some strict minded religious types condemn, this emotion occurs for those who *have an elevated desire toward a goal filled with tempting pleasure.*

Enthusiasm – Originally meaning "state of being inspired by God," this emotion occurs for those with *a lively and eager "interest in" or "admiration of" a purpose, activity or possibility.*

Curiosity – From an old saying dealing with the death of a cat, this emotion occurs *when people desire to know something which may or may not be confidential information.*

Eager*** – Originally meaning, "sour, sharp, impetuous," and often associated with metaphors about beavers, this emotion occurs for those who are *anticipating change and they desire this change to occur faster than its current pace.*

Sentimental**** – Derived from a Latin word meaning, "feeling," this *emotional state* occurs for those *whose emotions (and often not their reason) affect and guide their "interests, thoughts, views and attitudes."*

Exploration Opportunity:

1. How many other interest emotions can you find in the "Quiz Yourself" section of the appendix?

2. Which specific interest emotions are you most likely to experience?

3. What do you usually have going on around you when these emotions come up?

4. Describe the following emotions: Wish, Hanker, Pine, Whimsy, Anxious, Ambitious, Indifferent

*　　*This is also a* **Social Emotion**
**　　*This is also a* **Pleasure Emotion**
***　*This is also an* **Anticipation Emotion**
**** *This is also an* **Echo Emotion** *and a* **Secondary Emotion**

INVESTMENT EMOTIONS

Investment Emotions* put forth something of <u>value</u> to the investor in order to promote, sustain, maintain, nurture or appreciate whatever or whoever is being supported by the investment.

Investment Emotions are **Value Emotions** which tell you that you have put something of yours or of yourself toward what or who is before you. *Investment emotions naturally engender* **Comfort Emotions.** By refining your awareness of this emotion, you help yourself to more easily recognize specific emotions within this category and thereby give yourself more information about that investment.

The emotions listed below are variations on the "investment" theme and have accompanying information that may help you have better understanding when that emotion occurs.

...

Love/Agape – Sometimes misinterpreted as "charity," this emotion occurs for people who *both choose to accept unconditionally what is before them*

and who willfully invest of themselves for the welfare of all involved.

Courage – Long associated with "lion-heartedness," this emotion occurs for people *willing to confront the danger, discord or discomfort they perceive and which they might normally avoid.* (*Possible opposite*: **Reluctant** and **Loath**)

Trust – Part of a phrase printed on most United States currencies, this emotion occurs for people who *believe specific conditions support their well-being.*

Faith – Based on "no concrete evidence for or against," this emotion occurs for people who *believe "by choice."*

Hope – Suspected to be akin to "hop" and suggesting a notion of "jumping to safety," this emotion occurs for those who *desire to believe specific outcomes can occur where uncertainty is existent.*

Hate** – Mixed with pleasure and pain, this emotion occurs for those who *experience so much inner distress that they gladly invest thought, word or deed in attempts to create personal relief by imagining or bringing forth misfortune to others.*

Exploration Opportunity:

1. How many other investment emotions can you find in the "Quiz Yourself" section of the appendix?

2. Which specific investment emotions are you most likely to experience?

3. What do you usually have going on around you when these emotions come up?

4. Describe the following emotions: Schadenfreude, Forlorn, Saturnine, Malice, Care

*   *The opposite of* **Investment Emotions** *are* **Divestment Emotions,** *such as* **Forgiveness, Relief** *and* **Grief,** *which "divest" that which was originally invested in. These emotions also naturally engender* **Comfort Emotions.**

** *This can also be a* **Secondary Emotion**

3. CHANGE – Anticipation, Danger, Loss

Change Emotions relate to the occurrence or anticipation of change and transformation

Change Emotions tell you that transformation has occurred or may occur. These emotions give you information about how you perceive the change (or possible change) before you. **Anticipation Emotions,** *a subcategory of* **Change Emotions,** focus specifically on *perceived shifts in positive or negative potentials.*

The emotions listed below are variations on the "change" theme and have accompanying information that may help you have better understanding when that emotion occurs.

...

Surprise – Literally meaning "to over take," this emotion occurs for those who *didn't expect something to occur and it did! A surprise is considered either pleasant or unpleasant depending on what the "something" is and on what your perception of it is.*

Shock – A derivative of the word "strike" and meaning "heavy blow, unpleasant surprise," this emotion occurs for those who *didn't expect an unpleasant occurrence.*

Anxious* – Often associated with the "wringing of hands" and a precursor to an event, this emotion occurs for those <u>*anticipating change,*</u> *often with apprehension and uneasiness about future uncertainties.*

Apprehension* – From the Latin root meaning, "take hold of" or "to seize," this emotion occurs for those <u>*anticipating undesirable change*</u> *and who remain "focused on" or "seized by"(obsessed) thoughts involving this* <u>*anticipation.*</u>

71

Worry* – Originally meaning, "to strangle," this emotion occurs for those who are *focused on imagined or anticipated changes* beyond their control.

Dread* – Often surrounded by ominous overtones, this emotion occurs for those who *perceive change is about to happen and have an intense reluctance to face or confront the situation.*

Anger – Originally meaning "narrow" and associated with anguish, this emotion occurs for those *called to action to protect and/or cause change.*

Exploration Opportunity:

1. How many other change emotions can you find in the "Quiz Yourself" section of the appendix?

2. Which specific change emotions are you most likely to experience?

3. What do you usually have going on around you when these emotions come up?

4. Describe the following emotions: Startle, Astonish, Bewilderment, Anticipation, Excitement, Restless, Nervous, Presentiment

* *These are more specifically* **Anticipation Emotions**

DANGER EMOTIONS

Danger Emotions relate to potential harm that is present or will occur.

Danger Emotions are a subcategory of **Anticipation Emotions** which give you information about how you perceive that potential.

The emotions listed below are variations on the "danger" theme and have accompanying information that may help you have better understanding when that emotion occurs.

...

Concern – From a root word meaning, "mingle," this emotion occurs for those *with a blend of interest, uncertainty and apprehension.*

Cautious – From a root-word meaning, "to be on one's guard," this emotion occurs for those who *exercise forethought to minimize perceived danger.*

Fear – From an Old English noun, meaning, "sudden terrible event, danger" (and often an adrenaline pumping experience), this emotion occurs for those who *perceive present or future danger.*

Insecure* – From the root meaning, "not without care," this emotion occurs for those *perceiving vulnerability to potential harm and a lack of safeguards or assurance.*

Alarm – Originally a "call to arms" from an Old Italian phrase "to the weapons!" this emotion occurs for those *with a sudden and intense awareness of immediate danger.*

Terror – From a root-word meaning, "shake with fear" and "to frighten," this emotion occurs for those who *experience intense fear, often to the point of restricting the ability to take action.*

Panic – Originally meaning, "terror caused by the god Pan," and often characterized by behavior toward a perceived overwhelming danger, this emotion occurs for those who *exhibit "out of control," useless and often disorderly activity.*

Aghast – From the root word meaning, "to frighten," this emotion occurs for those *shocked by terror, amazement or horror.*

Exploration Opportunity:

1. How many other danger emotions can you find in the "Quiz Yourself" section of the appendix?

2. Which specific danger emotions are you most likely to experience?

3. What do you usually have going on around you when these emotions come up?

4. Describe the following emotions: Apprehension, Timidity, Intimidation, Sluggishness, Misgiving, Wary, Foreboding, Faintheartedness, Trepidation, Vulnerable, Circumspect, Chary, Anxious

*   *This is also a* **Lack Emotion**

LOSS EMOTIONS

Loss Emotions relate to the experience of loss.

Loss Emotions are **Change Emotions** which tell you that something or someone is gone and no longer in its usual place. These emotions give you information about how you perceive your situation and how that loss affects you.

The emotions listed below are variations on the "loss" theme and have accompanying information that may help you have better understanding when that emotion occurs.

...

Despair – From the root word meaning, "no hope," this emotion occurs for those who *believe there is no possibility for a desirable outcome.*

Sad / Sadness – A word associated with the common root word for "saturate and satiate," this emotion commonly occurs for those who, at some level, *recognize they have experienced a loss.*

Woe – Meaning "loss," this emotion occurs for people *experiencing stressful or painful loss.*

Melancholy – From the root word meaning, "black bile," this emotion occurs for those who *have recognized a loss and are deeply pensive (lost in thought).*

Disappointment – Derived from the phrase "to be removed from an appointed office or position," this emotion commonly occurs for those who *have an appointment broken or an expectation not met.*

Depression – Sometimes referred to as "anger turned inward" or the fourth stage of the grieving process, this emotion occurs for those *experiencing a loss or change – whether it is recognized or not.* (It typically shows itself through low energy, low motivation, low concentration, low focus and isolation – with little or no conscious healing of the loss or adaptation to the change.)

Grief* – Akin to the word "grave," based on the meaning "heavy, weighty" and arising during the fourth stage of the grieving process, this emotion occurs for those *adapting and healing mentally and emotionally from a loss or change.*

Exploration Opportunity:

1. How many other loss emotions can you find in the "Quiz Yourself" section of the appendix?

2. Which specific loss emotions are you most likely to experience?

3. What do you usually have going on around you when these emotions come up?

4. Describe the following emotions: Heartbreaking, Dejection, Lament, Doldrums, Gloomy

*   *This is also a* **Divestment Emotion** *and a* **Comfort Emotion**

4. DISCOMFORT – Lack, Dislike, Provocation, Pain

Discomfort Emotions relate to situations and conditions when one perceives oneself to be disempowered or unable to do anything about the situation. These emotions encompass many variations that all follow this theme.

Discomfort – Meaning "not with strength," this emotion occurs for those who perceive themselves to be *without the desired mental strength to support themselves to face what is before them.*

LACK EMOTIONS

Lack Emotions relate to missing elements.

Lack Emotions are **Discomfort Emotions** that tell you that something or someone is missing from where you believe it should be. These emotions give you information about how you perceive your situation and how these missing elements affect you.

The emotions listed below are variations on the "lack" theme and have accompanying information that may help you have better understanding when that emotion occurs.

...

Boredom – From the root meaning to create a hole mechanically, this emotion occurs for those *unfulfilled by or left empty by what is before them. (Associated with:* **Ennui***)*

Awkward – Originally meaning, "Turning in the wrong direction," this emotion occurs for people who are *unsure and who lack confidence in their abilities.*

Numb – Meaning "insensitive," this emotion occurs for those who *seek to shut themselves off from their emotions.*

Apathy – From the French "Apathes" meaning "without feeling," this emotion occurs for those who are *indifferent to whom or what is before them.* (*Opposite*: **Passion**)

Dismay – Meaning, "deprived of power," this emotion occurs in people who *believe they are powerless over what is before them.*

Inadequate* – From the root meaning, "make unleveled or unequal" and a precursor to what some people call "**Toxic Shame**," this emotion occurs for people who *perceive their efforts to be "insufficient & not good enough."*

Exploration Opportunity:

1. How many other lack emotions can you find in the "Quiz Yourself" section of the appendix?

2. Which specific lack emotions are you most likely to experience?

3. What do you usually have going on around you when these emotions come up?

4. Describe the following emotions: Cheerlessness, Indifference, Despondent, Passivity, Vulnerable, Stoic, Despair, Morose, Hopeless, Pusillanimity, Pitiless, Regretless, Glum, Pessimistic, Unsure

*   *When this emotion is focuses on "personal value" and "personal being" where no hope is perceived to exist to change this reality, it may lead to the pain & dysfunctional behavior of* **Toxic Shame**.

DISLIKE EMOTIONS

Dislike Emotions relate to a partiality or preference against
specific people, situations, places or things.*

Dislike Emotions are **Discomfort Emotions** which tell you that a
bias against or a disfavoring has occurred. These emotions give
you information about how you view that bias or disfavoring.

The emotions listed below are variations on the "dislike" theme
and have accompanying information that may help you have better
understanding when that emotion occurs.

...

Dislike – Originally meaning, "displeasing," this emotion occurs
for those who *have a bias against specific people, places or things.*

Reluctance** – From the Latin root meaning, "to struggle
against," this emotion occurs for those with
an aversion, hesitation or unwillingness
toward what is before them.

Disgust – Meaning "not to one's taste," this
emotion occurs for people *repulsed by what
is before them.*

Spite*** – From an Old French word
meaning, "scorn, ill will," this emotion occurs for those *with petty
hatred and contemptuous <u>desires to defy</u> as shown with actions
which attempt to thwart, annoy & irritate.*

Enmity – From a French root word meaning, "enemy," this
emotion occurs for those *with active deep-seated ill will.*

Hostility – From the root word meaning, "stranger, enemy," this
emotion occurs for those *with opposition, antagonism or resistance
in thought or principle.*

Animosity – From the Latin Root "animus" meaning, "spirit, mind, courage, anger," this emotion occurs for those *with strong ill will and destructive desires.*

Loathe – From a word originally meaning, "hostile," this emotion occurs for those who *have disharmony in their thoughts or opinions.*

Antipathy – Meaning "opposite feel," this emotion occurs for those who *have an aversion toward or rejection of what is before them.*

Exploration Opportunity:

1. How many other dislike emotions can you find in the "Quiz Yourself" section of the appendix?

2. Which specific dislike emotions are you most likely to experience?

3. What do you usually have going on around you when these emotions come up?

4. Describe the following emotions: Antagonism, Animus, Aversive, Execrate, Disinclined

   *   **Dislike Emotions** *also have some* **Value Emotion** *aspects to them. People tend to dislike what they don't value.*
   **   *This is also an* **Echo Emotion** *and an* **Anticipation Emotion**
   *** *This is also an* **Investment Emotion**

PROVOCATION EMOTIONS

Provocation Emotions relate to disturbance.

Provocation Emotions are **Discomfort Emotions** which tell you that a disturbance has occurred. These emotions give you information about how you view that disturbance.

The emotions listed below are variations on the "provocation" theme and have accompanying information that may help you have better understanding when that emotion occurs.

...

Annoyance – From a Latin phrase, denoting "in hatred," this emotion occurs for people who *find what is before them grating.*

Indignation – From the French root word meaning "worthy," this emotion occurs for people who *believe what is before them deserves disdain.*

Exasperation – From the root word meaning "rough," this emotion occurs for those whose *circumstances and perceived ineffectiveness goads them to the point of possible taking injudicious action.*

Aggravation – Meaning "to burden," this emotion occurs for those *persistently burdened by what they do not like.*

Chagrin – From the French word meaning, "sad, vexed," this emotion occurs for those *disquieted or distressed by humiliation, disappointment or failure.*

Impatience* – The opposite of "willingness to wait," this emotion occurs for people *irritated by having to <u>wait unnecessarily</u> for what they want.*

Tetchy – From a root meaning, "habit" and commonly mistaken for a slang word for "touchy" due to semantic commonality, this emotion occurs for those *irritably or peevishly sensitive to their focus.*

Vexatious – From a Latin root meaning, "to agitate, trouble," this emotion occurs for those *dealing with trouble, agitation and distress.*

Exploration Opportunity:

1. How many other provoking emotions can you find in the "Quiz Yourself" section of the appendix?

2. Which specific provoking emotions are you most likely to experience?

3. What do you usually have going on around you when these emotions come up?

4. Describe the following emotions: Irritable, Crabby, Distraught, Cross, Choleric, Cranky, Antagonistic, Irascible, Impatient, Irk, Testy, Touchy, Care, Restless, Agitation

*   *This is also an* **Anticipation Emotion**

PAIN EMOTIONS

Pain Emotions relate to unwanted or stressful mental states and general or specific distress.

Pain Emotions are **Discomfort Emotions** that tell you that distress has occurred. These emotions give you information about how you perceive that distress.

The emotions listed below are variations on the "pain" theme and have accompanying information that may help you have better understanding when that emotion occurs.

...

Hurt – Borrowed from a French word meaning "knock" and a synonym for "injure," this emotion occurs for people who *experience harm, abuse or violation.*

Pain – From the Greek root word meaning, "punishment or penalty," this emotion occurs for people who are *"stuck" and who may be resisting something.*

Suffer – Originally meaning, "to hold up from underneath; to sustain," this emotion occurs for those *enduring or undergoing a sustained unpleasant situation.*

Misery – Originally, meaning, "wretched," this emotion occurs for those with *great distress and unhappiness. It is usually associated with poverty or affliction.*

Torment – Meaning, "torturous twisting," this emotion occurs for people who *suffer mentally by the "painful twisting" of their thoughts.*

Anguish – Related to the root word for "Anger," this emotion commonly occurs for those *in chronic torment.*

Agony – Meaning "struggle, anguish," this emotion occurs when people *physically suffer from intense torment.*

Angst* – Borrowed from a German word denoting "intense emotional strife," this emotion occurs for those *with sharp painful anxiety, apprehension, or dread. It may accompany depression.*

Exploration Opportunity:

1. How many other pain emotions can you find in the "Quiz Yourself" section of the appendix?

2. Which specific pain emotions are you most likely to experience?

3. What do you usually have going on around you when these emotions come up?

4. Describe the following emotions: Solace, Dread, Revulsion, Anxious

*   *This is also an* **Anticipation Emotion**

5. COMPLEX – Mixed, Saturation, Social, Echo, Secondary, Ed

Complex Emotions relate to emotional experiences containing two or more concurrent influences.

Examples of this include:

1. overlapping or composite situations
2. too much information
3. past situations influencing current situations
4. situations influenced by other people
5. conflicting situational information
6. information compounding other information

MIXED EMOTIONS

> *Mixed Emotions relate to the occurrence of two or more concurrent activities, thoughts or states.*

Mixed Emotions are **Complex Emotions** which tell you that you have two or more things occurring simultaneously. If you can imagine tuning for a radio station and getting not one but two or more at the same time, this is very much like what occurs with mixed emotions. These emotions give you information about how you perceive your situation and how these things affect you.

The emotions listed below are variations on the "mixed" theme and have accompanying information that may help you have better understanding when that emotion occurs.

...

Ambivalence – Meaning, "both states," this emotion occurs for those who *have two or more contradictory and simultaneous emotions toward an object, person, or action.*

85

Confusion – Meaning, "pour together" or "to mix up, fail to distinguish," this emotion commonly occurs for those who *can't make sense out of a situation*. (*Closely related to* – **Flummox, Perplexity** *and* **Bewilderment**)

Doubtful – Meaning, "waver, be uncertain" and based on the word "duo," to illustrate the wavering between two possibilities, this emotion commonly occurs for those who *do not want to believe what is before them.*

Suspicious* – From the Latin root wood meaning, "to look at distrustfully," this emotion occurs for people who *doubt their trust in something or someone and <u>anticipate</u> some form of harm.* (*Also* – **Leery**)

Déjà Vu – Borrowed from a French word meaning, "already seen," this emotion occurs for people who *have a strong sense of familiarity with an event, thing, location, or person when they know that no familiarity exists.*

Exploration Opportunity:

1. How many other words can you find in the "Quiz Yourself" section of the appendix to express mixed emotions?

2. Which specific mixed emotions are you most likely to experience?

3. What do you usually have going on around you when these emotions come up?

* *This is also an* **Anticipation Emotion**

SATURATION EMOTIONS

Saturation Emotions relate to extreme situations.

Saturation Emotions are **Complex Emotions** that tell you that something, someone, or a situation is beyond your ability to deal with effectively. These emotions give you information about how this affects you.

The emotions listed below are variations on the "saturation" theme and have accompanying information that may help you have better understanding when that emotion occurs.

...

Overwhelm – Referring to a nautical term meaning, "sunk boat," this emotion commonly occurs for those who *have too much occurring at once.*

Rage – From the Latin Root "Rabies" meaning, "Madness, frenzy, fury," this emotion occurs for those *experiencing a high degree of anger. (It is often accompanied by strong desires to "strike out" at that which is perceived to be the reason for the rage.)*

Fright – From a prehistoric German root word meaning "afraid" and implying "sudden shock and paralysis coupled with the perception of danger," this emotion occurs for those *overwhelmed with a sudden and startling awareness of immediate danger.*

Consternation – From the root word meaning, "Overcome, confuse, dismay," this emotion occurs for those *overcome with sudden alarming amazement or dread that results in utter confusion.*

Frustration – Meaning "in error, in vain, useless," this emotion occurs for those *experience the result of futile actions and, more specifically, those actions taken in hope of causing certain outcomes and not having those desired outcomes occur.*

Ecstasy – Originally referring to "someone out of his/her mind," this emotion occurs for those *overwhelmed by delight.*

Awe – Often used in expressions referring to experience of deity, this emotion occurs for those *overwhelmed by wonder, admiration, respect, dread, and/or reverence.*

Rapture – From the Latin root meaning, "to seize by force" this emotion occurs for those *overwhelmed by intense bliss or utter delight.*

Exploration Opportunity:

1. How many other saturation emotions can you find in the "Quiz Yourself" section of the appendix?

2. Which specific saturation emotions are you most likely to experience?

3. What do you usually have going on around you when these emotions come up?

4. Describe the following emotions: Fury, Wrath, Transport, Exasperation, Mad

SOCIAL EMOTIONS

Social Emotions relate to the interplay & influence of others on us.

Social Emotions are **Complex Emotions** which tend to occur because of the involvement or influence of others. These emotions give you information about how you perceive your situation and how these "others" affect you.

The emotions listed below are variations on the "social" theme and have accompanying information that may help you have better understanding when that emotion occurs.

...

Understanding* – Meaning, "foundational knowing," this subtle emotion occurs for those who *"connect with" or who are "aware of" what is supportive or foundational in a given situation.*

Sympathy –
Meaning, "feeling with," this emotion commonly occurs for those who *are aware of the emotional state or situation of another and whose own similar emotional patterns are affected by this.*

Empathy – Meaning, "in feeling," this emotion commonly occurs for those who *picture themselves being in the same situation as another, thereby generating emotions that being in that situation would normally promote.*

Compassion** – Meaning, "suffering together," "with suffering" or "mutual suffering," this emotion commonly occurs for those *moved to take action to assist in another's struggles.*

Ruth – Borrowed from the name of a Biblical character, this emotion commonly occurs for those who *shift from stern indifference or apathy to compassion in regards to another's plight.* (*Opposite*: **Ruthless**)

Pity* – Coming from the Latin root for "pious" and often used in a derogatory or belittling fashion, this emotion commonly occurs for those who *recognize the loss experienced by others.*

Embarrassment – Based on the word "embargo" and meaning, "to put behind bars," this emotion commonly occurs for those who are *unprepared to deal with that which is before them and who don't want others to see them this way.*

Humiliation – Often erroneously confused with **humility** and **shame**, this emotion occurs for people who *perceive an unwanted and obvious degradation of their personal value in the eyes of others.*

Revengeful* – Sharing a common root with the word "vindicate," this emotion occurs for those who *have a strong drive to retaliate or get even for a perceived offense.*

Schadenfreude – A German compound word meaning, "damage, harm + joy," this emotion occurs for those who *take pleasure in the misfortune of others.* (*English equivalent:* **Epicaricacy** *and related in meaning to* **Sadistic**)

Forgiveness* – From a Latin "calqued word" or "loan translation" (a word or phrase borrowed from another language by literal, "word-for-word" or "root-for-root" translation), whose underlying intent means, "to give wholeheartedly," this emotion occurs for those *pardoning an offense.****

Lonely**** – Coming from the compound word "all one" this emotion occurs for those who *want but lack companionship.*

Exploration Opportunity:

1. How many other social emotions can you find in the "Quiz Yourself" section of the appendix?

2. Which specific social emotions are you most likely to experience?

3. What do you usually have going on around you when these emotions come up?

4. Describe the following emotions: Encouragement, Mercy, Merciful, Merciless, Kindness, Pitiless, Solicitous, Ruthless, Commiseration, Consideration, Sullen

*   *People also direct these emotions toward themselves.*
**   *This is also an* **Investment Emotion**
***   *This is also a* **Divestment Emotion** *and a* **Comfort Emotion**
**** *This is also a* **Lack Emotion**

ECHO EMOTIONS

*Echo Emotions continually come back (or echo) because the
message the emotion has to offer has not been acted upon,
acknowledged, or validated so closure can occur.*

Echo Emotions are **Complex Emotions** which tell you that
something is unresolved. While Echo Emotion may connect you
to other unresolved emotions, those other unresolved emotions
don't support the underlying message the "echo" emotion is trying
to give you. Echo emotions give you information about how this
affects you.

Divestment Emotions differ from **Echo Emotions** in that
*Divestment Emotions primarily focus on letting go of what was
originally invested in.* When **Echo Emotions** resolve, **Divestment
Emotions** frequently follow because the message of the echo
emotion was acted upon.

The emotions listed below are variations on the "echo" theme and
accompany information for each that may help you have better
understanding when that emotion occurs. Although any emotion
may "echo," the following emotions *tend to linger until resolved.*

...

Resentment – Literally meaning, "feel again" or "feel back," this
emotion commonly
occurs for those who
*have unresolved
emotions, usually due
to harm or discord
which has occurred
or is believed will
occur.*

Regret – This emotion occurs for those who *have unresolved sadness and literally means, "to weep again or to weep back,"* indicating an unresolved loss.

Remorse – Meaning, "to bite again" or "to bite back," and implying that something within is being "eaten away," this emotion commonly occurs for those who *have unresolved and possibly corrosive guilt.*

Bitterness – Implying, "distasteful and distressing," this emotion occurs for those *experiencing resentment to the point of pain.*

Rancor – From a root wood meaning, "Stinking, putrid," this emotion occurs for those *holding a grudge – a bitter, long-lasting resentment coupled with deep-seated ill will.*

Exploration Opportunity:

1. How many other echo emotions can you find in the "Quiz Yourself" section of the appendix?

2. Which specific echo emotions are you most likely to experience?

3. What do you usually have going on around you when these emotions come up?

4. Describe the following emotions: Repentance, Contrition, Bitterness, Mournful, Acrimony, Reluctance, Sentimental

SECONDARY EMOTIONS

Secondary Emotions find their support in underlying primary emotions.

Secondary Emotions are **Complex Emotions** that tell you that you have other underlying emotions at the core of your experience and you should look at these to have better understanding of what you actually perceive.

Example: *Anger is a secondary emotion. When you look below the surface of the anger, you may find any one (or more) of the following emotions:*

- Fear
- Guilt
- Love
- Hate
- Pride

- Shame
- Sadness
- Disgust
- Shock
- Surprise

- Jealousy
- Annoyance
- Embarrassment
- Disappointment
- Hurt / Pain

There may be a host of other emotions supporting the occurrence of anger. Any one of them can trigger the generation of anger – *a call to action to protect and/or cause change.*

What's important to remember is that when a secondary emotion is present such as anger, it is highly likely that at least one underlying emotion supports it. When that underlying emotion resolves by being addressed and dealt with honorably, the emotion "anger" will also find resolution.

Other emotions, in addition to anger, may show up as secondary too.

Example: *When Becky experiences frustration, she knows that it's an underlying desire that always drives her frustration. Her desire is not presently satiated due to ineffective actions on her part. Her frustration intensifies to communicate this to her. She knows that her frustration will go away once her underlying desire is satiated. She knows that her desire is strong and if it's not satiated, her desire may elevate from frustration to anger. She focuses herself on taking actions that are more effective.*

Echo Emotions *point you toward something unresolved that is not presently before you. It is a "past tense" situation.*

With **Secondary Emotions**, *there is always at least one underlying emotional also before you that supports the secondary emotion. It is a "present tense" situation.*

Exploration Opportunity:

1. How many other secondary emotions can you find in the "Quiz Yourself" section of the appendix?

2. Which specific secondary emotions are you most likely to experience?

3. What do you usually have going on around you when these emotions come up?

4. Describe the following emotions: Compassion, Frustration, Vengeance, Hate, Sentimental

WHAT'S WITH "ED?"

Words that you use to express emotions that end in "ed" are called **"Ed" Emotions.** They are **Complex Emotions** and are most often outwardly focused. They most always explain _why_ you have the emotion that you experience but never truly tell you directly the _actual emotion_ itself. When you think and express "ed" emotional words, you have yet to own the true emotion and hence it's easy to view the emotions as coming from an outside source.

Example: I'm feeling abused (ending is "ed")
Why: Because I'm _being_ abused
Connection to the past: Prior experience of being abused
True Present Emotion: Hurt

Another aspect of using "ed" words is that they express emotional experiences that may often relate the current experience to similar experiences in the past.

The expression in the example above answers "_why_" you "feel what you feel" but it does not reveal the actual _emotion_ you are experiencing. _The way you use words may trap you. With "ed" words, you don't have an emotion; the emotion has you!_

Further examination reveals the true emotion is "hurt." It occurs due to violation or harm _from the abuse._ When you say you "feel abused," you are jumping directly to the stimulus and don't "own" the true emotion you are experiencing.

YOU ARE NOT ALONE

People who generate "ed" pattern emotional expressions often focus on an outside cause for what they are experiencing internally. *Another example of this is a person being "scared."* The actual emotion is "fear" but because of the focus, the blame for that fear is on something other than the person who is generating it. Most often, you hear people saying "you scared me!" or "it scared me" rather than "I feel fear." There is a difference! "What is the difference?" you ask.

The difference, most of the time, is one of *ownership*.

The difference between feeling "abused" and experiencing the emotion "hurt" is that the first word focuses outward toward the cause of a violation. It is more inclined to answer the question *"why"* a person experiences what they do. *(It also subtly communicates possible "victim-hood.")*

Words ending with "ed," when used to express "feelings," are almost always used in this way. It's extremely important to take "ownership" of the emotion in order to be empowered by it.

The second word "hurt" focuses on the *emotional affect* of that violation and the person who generates that *energy pattern* "owns" the emotion in total.

Exploration Opportunity:

1. Look at the appendix on page 139 for a list of "**Ed's Words**."

2. For each "ed" word, ask yourself what emotion is actually occurring.

IV. Make Your Best Choices – Maturity

*What do you do with
what you know you're receiving?*

***

*It is not enough to "know."
Mature people take what they know
and apply it toward what is
useful, valuable and meaningful
for themselves and others.*

*Maturation requires a commitment
to continually perfect
what must be perfected
to bring about worthwhile outcomes.*

A. Receive & Decode Your Message

Up until now, the focus of this book has been on understanding the basics of emotions:

1. What emotions are
2. What they are not
3. How they manifest themselves
4. What they overtly and subtly communicate

The next focus of this book is how to:

1. Connect with your own messages
2. Understand the connections
3. Develop even stronger connections
4. Make better choices as a result

To help you do all this there are specific steps and exercises presented herein that will help you make your best choices.

After you complete this section, you should have the ability to decode any emotion you come across, and much more.

Here are those steps.

Step 1: Take Ownership

There is nothing more empowering than taking ownership of what is rightfully yours. This includes emotions!

The first step toward making a supportive choice is to take ownership of what you experience. No one else 'feels what you feel' and no one else "generates the emotions driving your body shift."

Start by saying something like: *This is something that I am experiencing because of what I think.*

Deed
Of Ownership

WARNING: *You might try to dismiss what you experience. Others may also make effort to dismiss what you have experienced by dismissing what you think. Do not dismiss what you sense! Do not dismiss what you think. Take ownership!*

Exploration Necessity:

1. What emotions of yours are you most likely to dismiss?

2. What thoughts of yours are you most likely to dismiss, especially when others encourage you to be dismissive?

3. What are the patterns of these dismissals?

4. When warranted, what can you do to better own your thoughts and emotions?

5. Write this out!

Step 2: Identify Your Emotion

If you don't know which emotion is present, you're off to a fuzzy start. By identifying the emotion(s) you experience, you make a conscious connection with how you perceive your experience.

Keeping this in mind, let's take a look at the emotions that you listed in the previous step and apply all that you have learned from previous chapters to make sure that what you have identified is a genuine emotion. If it is not, then make effort to find the emotion that best exemplifies what you expressed as an emotion in the previous step.

If you did not write down any emotions in the previous step, identify an emotion that you would really like to explore. You might want to

focus on an emotion that you frequently experience and that you would like to know more about. Whatever emotion you choose, make sure that you truly are interested in knowing more about it.

Exploration Opportunity:

1. What emotions of yours would you like to know better?

2. Write this out!

Step 3: Explore Your History

An empowering way to connect with your emotions is to look at your history with any one specific emotion. By examining the events surrounding emotional occurrences, you'll be much more likely to know what conditions need to exist for an emotion to occur.

Before you draw a false conclusion here, please remember that the conditions do not cause your emotion; your thoughts about the conditions do.

Once you have identified an emotion to explore, create a list of common events, people and conditions in which this emotion usually occurs.

Example: *Common events, people and conditions when Zack experiences "fear" – threatening tone of voice, odd look in the eyes, unpredictable body movements, low lighting, quick pace of the environment, many strangers, and flashes of light which accompany loud noises.*

Exploration Opportunity:

1. Make your best effort to describe all the elements (events, people and conditions) you can and the potential impact these elements might have, will have, or do have on you as a result.

2. Write this out!

Step 4: Identify the Feelings

Part of getting in touch with your emotions is to clearly identify, what occurs to your body because of a generated emotion. By knowing what usually occurs, you'll be better able to notice the shift in your body when it happens.

You can do this for the emotion that you selected in the previous step. Create a list of body sensations and reactions that usually occur when this emotion and these elements (events, people and conditions) occur. Make sure you write this out and include everything that you sense as your body shifts because of the emotion.

My Sensational List

Continuing with the Example of Zack Experiencing "Fear": *pulse racing, temperature rise, sweats, tension in specific body area: gut, neck, back, legs, chest, shallow breathing or holding breath, dry eyes, nervous twitches, eye muscles tight, speaking pitch rises, stuttering, dry throat, facial flush, tingle in the back of the neck.*

Once you know what normally occurs for you, with your chosen emotion, you can create similar lists for other emotions to help you better identify the sensations that occur when an emotion generates.

Exploration Opportunity:

1. Identify your feelings (body sensations).

2. Write this out!

Step 5: Explore Your Perception

*Every emotion has a message attached to it. Once you've
identified the emotion and the resulting body sensations, the next
step is to decode the message.*

To identify the primary message or indication of the emotion,
merely "boil" down into one or two words,
all the words, phrases or sentences you
would normally use to describe what you
perceive is occurring.

Sometimes the best way to do this is just ask
the following question:

*What is it that I perceive (as in "think or believe is
occurring or will occur") when this emotion occurs?*

Example: QUESTION – *What is it that Zack perceives when
he experiences "**fear?**"*
ANSWER – *He perceives "**danger.**"*

By asking yourself this simple question about your chosen
emotion, you have an opportunity to specifically examine what you
perceive in that moment, or as you reflect back to a time when that
emotion occurred.

Exploration Opportunity:

1. What do you perceive when you experience the emotion in
    question?

2. Write this out!

Step 6: Identify the Message

From our previous example using "fear," it is clear that when this emotion occurs, the perception is "danger."

The message communicated by Zack's thoughts at the most rudimentary level is:

Zack perceives that there is danger before him.

Because Zack perceives danger, his body energy pattern transforms to tune his body toward being better able to deal with what he perceives.

Zack's body itself transforms because the energy transforms it. You, like Zack, will learn with persistent, patient practice to notice this transformation by sensing the shift.

As you perceive additional information that supports your original perception, this may also affect your voluntary behaviors even to the point that those around you may notice this too.

All this because Zack (you) received a basic message:

DANGER

Exploration Opportunity:

1. Identify the message of your chosen emotion.

2. Write this out!

Step 7: Develop Your Question

Many people already know on some level when they "feel" a shift and label the emotion that causes the shift accordingly.

Developing this simple question gives you an opportunity to train yourself to ask it of yourself. Your question should be designed to help you better deal with whatever is before you. Because of this effort, you will be able to mobilize your best thinking so you can deal with your life more effectively and efficiently.

The Heart of a Question is the Quest.

Once you have gone thorough all these steps and arrived at the message, the next step is to ask yourself the following simple question. Again, in this case, our example is "fear":

What <u>DANGER</u> do I perceive?

By asking this simple question, you open yourself up to looking at what is before you and examining what specifically is a danger to you. Without the help of this question (or something like it) to focus your energies to deal with the danger(s), fear frequently has the consequence of causing you to think nebulously or to not think at all. This lack of effective thinking leads to a lack of effective action. By identifying the danger or dangers, you now have the ability to respond to them specifically and without any doubt.

Exploration Opportunity:

1. Develop specific questions for all the emotions you most commonly experience.

2. Write them out!

Step 8: Visualize Your Future

Here's a powerful step to nurture & support your efforts.

Create an "anchor" to use into your future. An anchor increases your tendency to think and do specific things, actions you want to do, when specific conditions occur.

HOW IT WORKS

You consciously create a memory of thinking and doing specific things when certain situations occur. Doing this allows you to draw from this memory when you need it most. The more real you make it and the more consciously you create it, the more it will be there to help remind you of what you need to do when the time is right.

Yes, this is "self-programming." You're about to "pre-program" yourself to take some foundational actions that will help you make your best choices into the future.

THE STEPS YOU HAVE BEFORE YOU ARE IMPORTANT

The more you expand upon them, the more your anchoring strengthens. It's up to you to go into detail.

PREPARATION NOTE

Create an environment where you can focus and where nothing will interrupt you.

Okay! Let's begin to anchor your Emotional Awareness!

1. Assure yourself that no matter what you imagine, you will remain safe throughout this exercise.
2. Imagine the elements occurring around you that you described in previous steps.
3. As you imagine these elements, become aware of how your body energy transforms by your imaginings.
4. As your body energy shifts, become aware of each telltale sensation changing in your body.
5. Affirm the emotions that you experience.
   a. **Example:** *Wow! I'm feeling "fear!"*
6. State overtly the message you're receiving.
   a. **Example:** I perceive danger.
7. State overtly the previous chapter's question.
   a. **Example:** *What danger do I perceive?*
8. Consciously examine your imaginary situation for any clue as to the possible dangers you perceive.
9. Based on what you have gathered from your imaginary situation, explore your best options & actions.

These are the basics. They will give you a strong start on what you want to accomplish. *Practice them daily* until you make them part of your life.

Exploration Opportunity:

1. Repeat this exercise with other situations that create the same emotion.

2. Repeat this exercise with other emotions that you commonly experience.

V. Transform Your Life – Legacy

The best is yet to come!

***

Commitment and mission share the same root meaning: "put, send" and "perpetuate."

*Should you want to perpetuate
what you have started,
you must "commit" to excel
in improving your emotional
awareness, clarity and maturity.*

*Your "mission" requires you
to deliberately venture
into areas where you can benefit
yourself and others.*

An Unbelievably Quick Review

The information presented in this book has even further uses for transforming your life.

This may not be obvious to you at first but if you examine the elements put forth in previous chapters, you might see how they all connect.

Before we go into a method you can use to create transformation, let's quickly review these elements and add a bit more to the mix that may not be immediately apparent.

Stage 1 – Thoughts: Thoughts occur in your bio-electrically based brains and present themselves, consciously or not, as the unified patterns of your individual Values, Interests, Perceptions, and Experiences.

Stage 2 – Emotions: These thought patterns create other patterns called emotions, which in turn affect the biochemistry of your physical body. Emotions are essentially message-oriented patterns that tune or shift your body's energy based on what your perception (your thoughts) of reality is. This tuning occurs automatically

Stage 3 – Sensations: These shifts in your body's energy patterns transform your body's chemistry. Your ability to sense these shifts depends on your immediate focus and overall sensitivity to what has shifted. The presence of other *chemicals, including hormone levels in both women <u>and men</u>, also influence this sensitivity!*

Stage 4 – Choices: Once these emotions manifest themselves, you have an opportunity to make a choice to take specific action based on this shift. This choice may occur consciously, unconsciously, subconsciously, overtly, or covertly. Your choice can also be informed, uninformed, misinformed or assumptive.

Stage 5 – Behaviors: Whatever the case, you will take some kind of action based on those choices and when you do, you manifest behavior. These patterns not only show themselves in your actions, they also shape your body language, your body tone and vocal intonation and your choice and formation of spoken words.

Stage 6 – Results: The behaviors you choose to do, in turn cause specific results, outcomes and consequences. These events are a directly or indirectly result of the behavior you manifested.

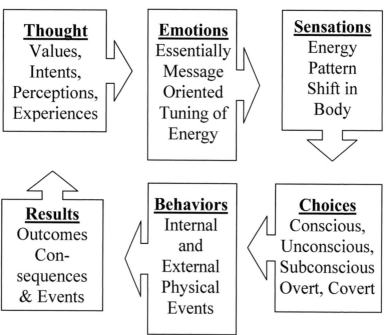

When these events occur, you might or might not think about them. It may not be conscious thoughts. Your thinking may not even be at a conscious level and it may at times involve assumptive thoughts. Whatever level of thought it takes, your values, intentions, perceptions, and experiences shape those thoughts.

Does this sentence sound like one you've read before? If you step back and take notice, you've already cycled around into the first stage again.

As you can see, the results you get are a consequence of the thinking you do, the choices you make and the actions you take. The rest of the information here lets you know the strong connecting background of the thought-choice-action-results chain.

Now that you consciously know how this chain works, you can use this information to examine the results of your thinking and determine how to best change the results by changing your thinking.

Additionally, by knowing which phase leads to the next, you can simply reverse the direction and ask yourself if you believe each phase helps to bring about what you want most. If it doesn't, merely examine what brought you to that stage. You can ascertain what you should change in the preceding stages to bring about the results you do want.

Exploration Opportunity:

1. What emotions would you like to better understand?

2. What situations would you like to be able to handle better?

3. What areas would you like to transform your life for the better?

4. Write these out! Then take each emotion through the process this chapter has presented to you. Write out your results and the new actions you will take to bring them about. Dream big but don't bite off more than you can chew at one time!

A. New Thoughts Make New Lives

Your life is a direct result of your thoughts and so are your emotions!

To transform your life (and hence your emotions), you must begin the process of creating the thoughts which will transform it. *New thoughts alone will not transform your life.* Only new thoughts – *which help bring about the results you want* – will change your life.

How can you make this occur? Start with examining your life results.

Stage 1 – Results: If you're current results don't please you and you want this to change, you must examine how your current behavior *brings about* those results.

As the old saying goes, "If you keep doing what you're doing, you'll keep getting what you're getting." To change your results, you must change your behavior toward more effective action.

In other words, you must take actions that influence how the desired results turn out for those actions to be deemed effective.

Before you do begin though, ask yourself what it is that you truly want. What end-in-mind do you really want to achieve? What would an acceptable outcome be? Dream Big! What would an exceptional outcome be? *Your results are within your control because of your behavior is too.*

Stage 2 – Behaviors: How do you know if your actions are effective? Just look at your results. Are you affecting your results by your choice of action? If so, how? If not, how? By evaluating your behavior, you should be able to determine your action-result connection. By examining your results, you might find ways to improve the actions you choose to take into the future.

Are you aware of actions that are more effective? Are you capable of taking such actions? What support activities do you need to be engaged in to best take the most effective actions to achieve your intended outcome? *Your behavior is a matter of your choice.*

Stage 3 – Choices: If your choice of action was not the best, then this should lead you to examine *how* you came to make your choice. You could start by asking yourself the following questions:

- Was my choice a fully informed choice?
- Was my choice a misinformed choice?
- Was my choice overt or covert?
- Did I consciously think about what I was about to do or was I doing it out of habit?
- Did I make my choice because of a "feeling?"
- Was my choice a *reaction* rather than a *response* to someone or something?

As you examine your choices, you may want to look at some other possibilities. How could your choice have been a better one? What choice would have led you to the best possible behavior to support what you truly want to be your result?

There are times when people truly want to avoid the results of their choices and actions. They usually refer to them as "consequences." The desire to avoid unwanted consequences is a natural one. People in situations like this often say, "They had no other choice." The reality is that this is an illusion. *There are always other choices* but these other choices as viewed as *unacceptable* because they represent unwanted consequences. People will summarily dismiss these choices as non-viable options and excuse themselves from those choices by saying that *there was no other choice other then the one they chose.*

Did you design any of your choices to avoid a consequence? To gain better control of your behavior, you must know how you go about making your choices. *Your options don't determine the choice you make; what you believe to be your acceptable options will determine what you choose.*

Stage 4 – Sensations: The more major a choice is, the more major the body sensations you'll have prior to when you make that choice. Minor sensations may precede minor choices. These sensations are what occur for you because of emotions shifting your body chemistry. The more aware you are of your body sensations, the more you will know when any shifts occur within your body.

What were you feeling just before you made your choice? Were you aware of any body cues? Were you conscious of how you felt? Were there any underlying sensation prior to you making your choice but you can't describe them?

It's important to improve your awareness of your body sensations because sensation is one of the quickest ways to tell when you've experienced a shift in an emotion. The sooner you gain that awareness, the more quickly you will be able to choose more effectively. If you have little or no awareness of your emotions and the messages they have for you then your ability to make effective choices, and achieve desired results, will be that much less. *Sensations that occur as an energy shift within a healthy body are a direct result of the emotions you have generated.*

Stage 5 – Emotions: Your ability to sense when your body has an energy shift is important. This skill will better assist you in knowing when an emotion shifts your body energy. This is doubly important because emotions both transform your body energy & inform you as to what you believe to be the situation before you.

115

The sooner you become aware of when this shift occurs, the more quickly you will know that there is something new about your reality that you can use to make your life better.

Every emotion occurs because of thought, directly or indirectly. When an emotion occurs, it is important to know as specifically as possible which emotion is occurring. This skill is important because it means you can readily track down the message the emotion tells you. It also lets you know how your body energy has transformed to tune itself to what you perceive to be your situation.

More importantly, emotion shifts also tell you that it would probably be to your advantage for you to do a reality check on your thinking.

Example #1: *Sydney experiences the emotion guilt. She knows that she has sent a message to herself that she has done something wrong. She then asks herself, "What did I do wrong?" Sydney quickly evaluates what brought her to the point where guilt occurred, reviewing her thoughts to "understand the connection between what she did and why it was wrong." Sydney swiftly assesses what she must do to take corrective action and make amends.*

Example #2: *Sydney examines the same situation again but more closely. She recalls that someone, whom she respects and likes, had told her that she had done something wrong. She had accepted her friend's statement as her reality. Sydney realizes that she had then automatically generated the emotion of guilt as a response to her perception. Upon further reflection, Sydney sees that her reasons, her thoughts and her emotion don't truly fit the situation. Because her thinking has changed, her emotion shifts to calm.*

Understanding the emotion that is occurring for you tells you directly the message you need to know so you can evaluate your situation with more clarity, accuracy and quickness and therefore make choices more supportive of what you perceive.

Transforming thought transforms emotions.

Stage 6 – Thoughts: This leads to what you think. If you're like most people, you've trained yourself to automatically think specific things under specific circumstances. (This is because it *requires work* to think non-routine thoughts. Many people prefer to not work that hard on their emotions, so they develop habits to fall back on.)

As has already been stated, any kind of thinking including automatic or habitual thought, still causes you to generate emotions supportive of those thoughts. Those emotions, even if the thoughts are so automatic they've become unconscious or reflexive, shift your body energy and you can still sense that shift in proportion to the shift's intensity & your focus. When this occurs, you routinely choose to respond to this shift in routine ways. That routine response brings about specific routine behavior and that behavior brings about specific routine results. *If you want to produce different results, you must think differently about what you perceive before you.*

Exploration Opportunity:

1. Use the illustration and information in this section to guide you. Create a list of results, outcomes and consequences that you want to change. Write down next to each item on the list what you would like to see change for that item.
2. Start at the result stage and work backward through the chain to the thoughts that brought about your original result. As you do, keep in mind that the links you made which brought about the original result have to change. So transform each link into something that directly supports what you want.

1. Connect with Your Dreams

There's a lot written about dream interpretation.

What you read here will be limited to some thoughts that you can explore should you choose to travel down this road.

You can gain a great deal of information about how you experience life from knowing the emotions that you generate when you dream.

As you diligently read this book and work through each of the opportunities, you should be able to use all the information you've learned and the skills you've developed to delve more effectively into your dreams.

KEEP IN MIND

How you perceive your world causes your emotions to occur. You should find your dream world to be no different *except for one thing.* You may find that carrying unresolved emotions from your waking life into your sleep can actually cause imagery that is much in tune with those waking emotions.

This occurs because your dominant emotional states during your waking hours heavily influence your dreams so that your mental imagery becomes a projection "movie screen" making effort to have you "see" what you were experiencing emotionally and feeling physically when you were awake.

Of course, you already know that it's your thoughts that cause your emotions, even if they are below conscious level. Your subconscious thoughts "want" to tell you what you perceive, to literally "make you aware." They project imagery within your dreams to help you get the message. *This occurs especially if you chose to ignore or deny what was right before you when you were awake.*

Yes! Emotions influence your dreams and dreams influence your emotions. Knowing this critical key will help you make connections you need to better interpret your dreams and better know your thoughts.

Here are some important questions to ask yourself when tuning into your dream world:
 1. What are the dominant emotions that occur during dreams at any one specific point?
 2. What are the images generated at those points?
 3. What were the dominant thoughts and perceptions in the dream just prior to an emotion becoming evident?
 4. What were the transitional steps? IE: What image- thought-perception-body-feeling-emotion chain occurred?
 5. What do the messages the dream emotions tell you about your reality?
 6. What might you conclude from becoming more aware of this information?

Example – *The following sequence occurred for one dreamer:*
 1. *Perceive: Fun scene; Experience: Joy; Body Sense: heart pounding evident even in dream state*
 2. *Perceive: Potential problem; Experience: Concern*
 3. *Perceive: Danger; Experience: Fear; Body Sense: heart pounding evident in dream state*
 4. *Perceive: Threat; Experience: Alarm; Body Sense: heart pounding evident in dream state*
 5. *Perceive: Unwillingness to Deal; Experience: Cowardice; Body Sense: tight chest*
 6. *Perceive: Disconnect; Experience: Loneliness; Body Sense: lowering energy*

119

7. *Perceive: Willingness to Face; Experience: Courage; Body Sense: energy increases*
8. *Perceive: Active Engagement; Experience: Excitement; Body Sense: heart pounding evident in dream state*

What you can gather from the previous example is that a series of thoughts brought about specific emotions which created sensations within the body of the dreamer.

Equally, each body sensation creates conditions that trigger more thoughts thus creating further emotions that affect the body.

Should you choose to explore more of this for yourself, keep in mind that in a dream state, many factors influence your imagery, your thought, and your body sensations and in turn, these three all influence each other.

The major influencing factor though, is what you think since emotions come from thoughts, no matter how subtle those thoughts might be.

Exploration Opportunity:

1. Create and keep a "Dream Journal" and keep it by your bed. Use it to explore the emotions that you experience in your dreams. Write down both what you think about just before you experience the emotions and the emotions that follow.
2. Include any imagery and sensations that occur just prior to and after your thoughts. Ask yourself what message each emotion tells you about your dreamed situations.
3. Ask yourself if you experience any similar emotions during your waking hours. Include when those emotions first occurred. If so, what messages do these emotions tell you about your waking world?
4. *Write all this down as soon as possible! Dreams evaporate quickly – delays will alter your results!*

2. Find Higher Purpose

Four purposes for emotions were shared earlier in this book. This section will focus on the last purpose: *to send and receive basic messages between people and have thee messages contain greater clarity in the expression and communication of emotional content.*

Once you've honed your ability to know what emotion you're generating, the message you send yourself (and others), what you perceive, and the thoughts that create your emotions, use your expertise to hone your ability to be able to better "sense" the following in others:

1. The emotions they're most likely generating
2. The messages most likely communicated by their emotions
3. The reality they most likely perceive
4. The general thoughts they're most likely thinking

By having an ability to sense these things, you're more likely to have a reasonable understanding of how they see their world. Even if your "sense" isn't fully accurate, the other person will "sense" that you have an interest in them, their "feelings," and their perceptions. You will also be in a better position to take care of your own thinking so you don't react to the other person in some way that could be detrimental to your relationship.

Use your awareness beneficially! Based on what you can gather, what can you do to better the odds of improving your interactions with them? What can you do to validate their perceptions? What words can you offer? What things can you do to let them know you recognize the message they're giving themselves?

Truly, all this is may seem to be guesswork, but your guessing comes with some extremely strong backing. To improve your guesses, you can do reality checks on your conclusions to test how accurate they are. By reading this book and working through the exercises, you have educated yourself on some especially fundamental communication. By learning more – by improving your awareness about this most fundamental internal communication system – you have added to your ability to make better choices when situations arise. As you patiently practice to perfect your abilities, you'll develop clarity and understanding that supports you in doing just that.

Even though some of what you guess may not be accurate, you can develop ways to test your assumption. Know the different steps to take in order to develop a better understanding of what occurs within you. You can use these very same skills to communicate with others more effectively. Yes! Your personal awareness is particularly portable so your "guesswork" will improve through better self-knowledge and with further usage.

Along with detecting cues from others to be better able to understand how they perceive their world, you can communicate the same back to them in a more purposeful and deliberate way. Should you see a situation a certain way, you can ask questions that will help you better determine if what you see is accurate.

Exploration Opportunity:

1. **Behavioral Cues:** Look for cues and other telltales that others might give off about their emotional state. (Body language / Intonation of voice / Body tone / Word usage)
2. **Take your best guess** as to what emotions others generate.
3. **Test your assumptions.** What questions can you ask other people based on the emotion you believe they exhibit? (**Direct Questions:** Are you afraid? / What are you afraid of? **Indirect Questions:** What's the danger? / What danger do you perceive? / What's the worst thing that could happen? **Really Indirect Questions:** What's going on? / How are you feeling?)

3. Develop Emotion-Message-Thought Chains

When you perceive someone generating their own emotional process, being skilled with using EMT chains can give you a much greater chance of identifying what this person perceives. Knowing what the perception a person has will tell you much about how they see things.

Emotion-Message-Thought Chains help you to better prepare yourself for comprehending the underlying message and the basic thoughts behind any emotion whether you generate it yourself or you become aware of it in another person.

Here are a few examples of emotions, each with its possible messages and the most probable thought that created the emotion. Try them out. If you can come up with more likely message and thought combinations for yourself, then this book will have helped you do your best!

Each EMT Chain listed below is written in the following format:

The Emotion - The Primary Message from the Emotion
           - The thought that led to the emotion and can
             typically be found by answering the question:
             What do I perceive, anticipate or have?

                    ...

Here are some typical EMT Chains:

Anger	**- Protection & Change**
	- I want to protect and cause change.
Apathy	**- Lack of Interest**
	- I have no interest in this.
Awkward	**- Lack of Confidence/Comfort**
	- I have unsure-ness of my abilities.

Uncommon Sense about Everyday Feelings

Boredom	**- Emptiness**	
	- I have no inspiration from this activity.	
Confusion	**- Disorientation**	
	- I have not connected with something.	
Courage	**- Willing to Face**	
	- I have willingness to face danger.	
Despair	**- Lack of Hope/Confidence**	
	- I have no hope.	
Disgust	**- Dissatisfaction**	
	- I find this distasteful.	
Embarrass	**- Trapped on Display**	
	- I am not ready, nor do I want, to be seen.	
Empathy	**- Relating to Someone Else's Situation**	
	- I can relate to someone else's situation.	
Envy	**- Desire**	
	- I want something that someone else has.	
Epicaricacy	**- Pleasured by Someone Else's Misfortune**	
	- I have pleasure in someone else's misfortune	
Fear	**- Danger**	
	- I perceive danger.	
Grief	**- Healing**	
	- I am healing from a loss or change.	
Guilt	**- Transgression**	
	- I have transgressed a value or limit.	
Hurt	**- Harm/Violation**	
	- I am suffering due to harm, abuse or violation.	
Jealous	**- Desire/Rightful Ownership**	
	- I believe someone else has something that is mine.	
Joy	**- Satiation**	
	- I have my needs met.	
Lonely	**- Isolation From**	
	- I want companionship.	
Love	**- Held as Dear/Valued**	
	- I have high regard for this.	
Merry	**- High and Light Energy**	
	- I have a light heart and high spirit.	

Numb	- **Lacking Sense**
	- I have shut off my sensitivity.
Overwhelm	- **Swamped & Sunk, Hard to "Breathe"**
	- I am drowning in this event & cannot breathe.
Pain	- **Resistance/Stuck**
	- I have resistance to something.
Pride	- **Value**
	- I value something.
Regret	- **Weep Again**
	- I have not healed a loss.
Remorse	- **Bite again**
	- I have something that is eating at me.
Resent	- **Feel Again**
	- I have an unresolved emotion.
Sadness	- **Loss**
	- I have experienced a loss of something.
Serenity	- **Calm, Peace, & Acceptance**
	- I have okay-ness with this and I accept this.
Shame	- **Limitation**
	- I have limitations.
Shock	- **Unexpected/Unanticipated**
	- I did not expect this and I'm not okay with it.
Surprise	- **Unexpected/Unanticipated**
	- I did not expect this but I'm okay with it.*
Sympathy	- **Affected by Someone Else's Situation**
	- I have emotions influenced by another's situation.
Yearn	- **Aching Desire**
	- I want something so much that I ache.

Exploration Opportunity:

1. Create a list of emotions that you want to develop "emotion-message-thought" chains. Develop your own chains and refine them as you make discoveries and become more aware.

* *This is why we have surprise parties and not shock parties.*

125

4. Ask Powerful Questions

Develop your ability to ask powerful questions. You can often learn much by simply giving others opportunities to share.

Questions are rooted in a quest – a "seeking" – that gives you opportunity to explore with purpose. Each emotion offers you a chance to seek *purposely*, for others or for yourself.

Here are some examples of questions you could ask when the example emotions occur. Use them as a guide to develop other questions for yourself and others to use.

- **Anger:** What do you want to protect? What do you want to change?
- **Frustration:** What do you really want? What are you getting instead? What actions have you taken? What other actions would improve your odds?
- **Guilt:** What did you do wrong? What value or limit did you transgress? How can you correct this?
- **Hurt:** Who or what harmed or violated you?
- **Sad:** What was lost? What did you lose?

Exploration Opportunity:

1. Create a list of emotions that commonly occur for you and those you know.

2. Develop a set of powerful questions that you can when these emotions occur.

5. Recognize Dismissals

*Develop a rock solid awareness and vigilantly protect your reality
when dismissals attack your emotions.*

Emotional dismissals are verbal or non-verbal (body language)
statements that make effort to deny and/or change what you're
experiencing emotionally. You'll detect them best when you know
what to listen for or look for internally and externally. When
dismissals are delivered verbally, listen for phrases or sentences
with patterns similar to the following:

- *I can't understand why you're so miffed!*
- *You have no right to be angry, upset or jealous.*
- *You shouldn't feel that way.*
- *Don't get upset.*
- *Don't be angry or afraid.*
- *Don't feel bad or sad.*
- *Don't feel that way.*
- *I know how you feel.*

Each sentence makes effort to deny or change your emotional
experience or distract you from what you perceive. When you
recognize sentences like these, you can prevent a dismissal from
occurring. Here are two ways you can handle dismissals:

Example #1: *Deb experiences loss and has sadness. Jay say, "I'm
sad to hear of your loss." Deb snips angrily at Jay, "Why are you
sad?" If Jay recognizes that he has sympathy for Deb's situation,
he can say, "I care for your well being. Knowing you're sad
affects me." If Jay has empathy he can say, "I've suffered loss
before. I can relate to what you're going through."*

Example #2: *Meg is upset because she placed trust in someone who <u>violated</u> her trust. She realizes that she <u>may lose</u> a good friend as a result. It's clear that Meg <u>expected</u> more. She sees <u>how this affects her future relationship</u> with those involved. Meg understands the <u>danger</u> that the situation presents. She "feels" <u>compelled to minimize</u> the damage. Meg experiences a mix of many emotions (i.e. hurt, sadness, disappointment, anxiety, fear and anger.) The person before Meg says coldly, "Get over it. You're making too much of this." Knowing how her emotional cues fit into her experience tells Meg otherwise. It also tells her that the person speaking to her doesn't know (or doesn't care to know) the importance of Meg's situation to Meg. She could try to educate him but she realizes she can better take care of herself by putting her energy to more constructive use.*

Your emotions occur because of what you think. If self-talk or social talk makes effort to dismiss what you generate authentically, rethink your options. Your emotions tell you that something in your environment was important enough to cause a shift in your energy pattern. Will you ignore it or deal with it?

What must you do to safeguard what you're telling yourself?

Exploration Opportunity:

1. Create a list of the dismissals you hear most often.

2. Add the names from who you hear these dismissals.

3. Add how you normally react to them and why.

4. Explore what you can do in a different way to safeguard yourself in the future.

5. Create an action plan to draw from for when you are having dismissals occur.

6. Identify & Avoid Mean Games

One of the purposes of emotions is to help you understand and deal with reality more effectively.

If you involve yourself in systems, relationships or social situations, professional or personal, which consistently sabotage this purpose for emotions then you will experience the abuses which these systems create. The specific term that you can apply to these activities is "Emotional Abuse." It takes many forms and many descriptions. No brief writing could ever do full justice to the variety of abuses that actually occur. The intent of any short description, such as this one, is only to introduce and create awareness for the reader.

WHAT IS EMOTIONAL ABUSE? Emotional Abuse is the systematic wearing down (*or prevention of healthy development*) of a person's ability to comprehend and deal effectively with their reality.

It doesn't matter whether the abuse is intentional or not. The effects are the same. It plays with the many aspects of you that create and regulate your emotions; it attacks you at your very core – your thoughts (values, intentions, perceptions, experiences/memories) and your behaviors. The resulting turbulence affects your self-esteem, self-confidence, self-image, choices, relationship and all other aspects of life.

The purposes of emotions are to tune, validate, imprint and communicate. Any corruption of any of these purposes leaves you at a moderate to severe disadvantage in dealing with your reality effectively. In this respect, emotional abuse is counter-productive for anyone so targeted.

The purposes of emotional abuse range from fostering dependency to maintaining control, always at someone's expense. Once again, it doesn't matter if this is intentional or not. It sometimes occurs with an abuser having the best of intentions and no understanding of how the abuser's action causes harm.

HOW DOES IT OCCUR? You'll usually detect the presence of some form of inequity of power. Non-level playing fields allow those with more influence to both "make choices" and "take actions" to the disadvantage of others. When this occurs, the resulting "game" contains (these range from subtle to obvious): depreciation, disrespect or non-valuing behavior toward anyone they target as less influential. Emotional abuse can show up in any of the following forms: invalidation, violation, denial, unpredictability, minimizing, distortion, reframing, rejection, corrupting, ignoring, isolation, exploiting, blackmail, or deception.

WHAT ARE THE MAJOR CUES? First, when functioning properly, you will "feel" or "sense" body shifts caused by your emotions even before you're consciously aware of any abuse. Secondly, remember no matter what form it takes, *a lie is always at the core of emotional abuse.*

Abusers (even those who are unaware of being abusive) don't want the truth to be known or acted upon. They rely on distractions to sabotage the abused or those who might step in with effective actions to stop it. Abusers effectively create unnecessary and unwarranted situations where emotions (i.e. anger, fear, hurt & sadness) are experienced and possibly suppressed by the target. Most often the abused are so caught up in the effects that they fail to grasp & deal with these situations effectively. Abusers depend on the target's lack of awareness and their ineffective responses to perpetuate this abuse. They also have built up an elaborate system of excuses to support their actions should anyone suspect that abuse exists. *Sadly, both the abusers & the abused may not even be aware of the abuses; their behaviors have become habitually "normal" for them both.*

WHAT ARE THE LONG TERM EFFECTS? While this is not a comprehensive list, you can probably expect the following (or similar) results: *lowered self-esteem, reduced ability or desire for social bonding, general mistrust, insecurity & indecision, insensitivity to non-physical pain, hyper-vigilance & fear, more accepting of aggression (giving or receiving), eventual emotional "burn out" and failure to thrive.*

WHAT IS THE BEST PROTECTION? *The best primary defense is a strong and unshakeable emotional awareness.* Educate yourself on how emotional abuse occurs. Explore the many self-tests made available by counselors & self-help groups that assist others to effectively identify, understand & deal with emotional abuse. Look closely at any abuse tactics that have played out in your life. Explore healthy & functional ways to deal with situations where abuses occur.

If you believe you need help with this issue, sources of support in the form of books, websites, professionals and support groups exist locally and nationally. All that is required is being persistent and consistent in your efforts to find them until you do.

Exploration Opportunity:

1. Educate yourself, more fully, as to what constitutes abuse.
   a. Learn more about abuse characteristics.
   b. Learn more about what you can do to prevent abuse.
2. Identify the times, places, situations and people that most often create conditions that wear you down emotionally – for all the wrong reasons.
3. Clearly state anything that contributes to wearing you down, including any lack of support and unfair, unreasonable or harsh rules.
4. Create an action plan that you can depend on to safeguard yourself when these conditions occur.

131

7. Commit to Explore & Improve

MORE EXPLORATION

You have developed much emotional awareness for yourself. Now is the time to develop your skills.

Here are some actions you can do to venture out and become a *true master of emotional awareness:*

Continue to…

1. Be in touch with your emotions by using your body senses to detect emotional shifts.
2. Ask yourself what basic emotions you experience.
3. Seek out the basic message your emotions communicate to you. *Record this in a journal.*
4. Explore what these emotions communicate to you about how you perceive your world.
5. Explore the connection between your thoughts and your perception.
6. Examine the validity of your paradigms regularly.
7. Refine your process so that you can jump directly from the body sense to what you are thinking in general about your situation.
8. Create personalized EMT chains for use into the future.
9. Explore how your "gut feelings" tie into your emotions.
10. Develop your list of powerful questions for each emotion that you encounter. *Write these out for future reference!*
11. Test your assumptions and questions regularly and adjust them accordingly!

Process refinement speeds your ability to ascertain your situation and help you clarify your next steps.

FURTHER IMPROVEMENT STEPS

Your journey has only just begun. Even after you finish reading this book, you can take many more actions to improve your emotional awareness and your choices.

Here are a few of them that you can use to explore your emotions further:

1. Commit – Continue to increase and improve your emotional awareness.
2. Examine – How do you make judgments based on the emotions you generate.
3. Monitor – Closely examine your body sense subtleties!
4. Connect – Know what you "feel" now.
5. Intentions – Know what "end in mind" you desire.
6. Attentiveness – Monitor your actions.
7. Reprogram and Remove - Go back to page 14 and rework all those buttons you wrote about.
8. Track Record – Look at your past results. What do your past results tell you?
9. Track your emotions and your moods – Discover and uncover your emotion and mood cycles.
10. Journal – Take time to write out what you discover. Include your emotions and your moods.
11. Explore – How are your intuitions and your emotions linked?
12. Visualize – Take time to imagine constructive behavioral responses into your future.

Don't let your journey stop here. Put together a schedule to keep these activities sharp and full of life. If you think it will help, work with a partner, friend or coach to help further refine what you know so you can be of even greater benefit to yourself and others.

Above all – have fun!

VI. Appendix

*More than you
probably want to know!*

A. Some Rules to Remember

Emotional Causation Rule (Pages 15-16)
- The person who is generating the emotions (by his or her thinking) is the one who is causing the emotions.
- **Corollary #1:** The person generating them is solely responsible for the emotions generated.
- **Corollary #2:** The person generating them should be held accountable for any action they have taken, no matter what his or her excuse or others may suffer needlessly.

Emotional Paradigm Rule (page 5)
- Paradigms dictate how we perceive our world.
- **Paradigm Shift Example #1:** The world is flat; the sun revolves around it. → The world is round; it revolves around the sun.
- **Example #2:** Emotions are energy. → Emotions are patterns in the energy.

Emotional Reflection Rule: (Page 57)
- For every emotion, there is at least one possible reflective emotion.
  Examples:
  - Confidence | Timidity
  - Pleasure | Pain
  - Like | Dislike
  - Calm | Disturbance
  - Hope | Despair
  - Delight | Despise
  - Courage | Cowardice

Emotional Intensity Rule: (Pages 47-79)
- Emotional Intensity is a function of personal values, interests, perceptions and experiences.
- The relative intensity of an emotional experience is directly proportional to, and in the same direction as, the overall thoughts driving and supporting it.
- **Corollary:** The willingness to experience it dictates the upper limit of that intensity.

Emotional Duration Rule: (Pages 53-54)

- Unless unresolved or a recycling thought, emotion affects usually resolve within 90 seconds.
- Moods last far longer than emotions.
- Thought and body chemistry greatly affect moods.

Emotional Judgment Rule: (Pages 19-20)

- No matter how hard people may try to re-label a judgment word to imply that it is an emotion, they will fail in their efforts every time when you ask them to tell you how that word feels.
- **Examples:** Good, Bad, Fine, Okay, etc.

Emotional Rational/Logical Rule (Pages 21-22)

- Emotions, in and of themselves, are neither rational/logical nor irrational/illogical.
- **Corollary #1:** The person generating any specific emotion may or may not be using rational/logical thinking (consciously, unconsciously, or subconsciously) to bring about the perception and thinking that creates the emotion being generated.
- **Example #1:** It is rational/logical that a person will generate fear should that person be facing legitimately danger. Two people, both using logical conscious thinking, and experiencing the same event, have a high chance of generating differing emotions because of the likelihood that they each have differing perceptions of the event.
- **Example #2:** It's rational/logical that a person generates sadness should that person face legitimate loss.

Emotional Regulation Rule (Pages 50-53)

- Healthy and functional emotion regulation occurs when emotions serve their purpose.
- Unhealthy and dysfunctional emotion regulation occurs when emotions don't serve their purpose.
- **Corollary:** Some addictions are due to poor choices in emotion regulation behavior.
- **Example:** Anger motivated complains and actions serve no purpose if the complains and actions are in a direction that makes no difference toward causing change or causing protection. The anger will continue without serving the purpose it was intended to serve.

Emotional Button Rule (Pages 13-14)

- You're the only one who controls your "buttons."
- You cause your own emotions concerning others.
- You control no one else's buttons.
- **Corollary #1:** When you don't take ownership of your own "buttons," it's much easier for you to believe – falsely - that others push them and then you can blame others for what you generate.
- **Corollary #2:** Irresponsible people will try to convince you that you cause their emotions.

Emotional Dismissal Rule (Pages 127-128)

- People, whose perception leads them to "feel" threatened by what someone else's emotion says or indicates, make effort to dismiss all evidence supporting that emotion.
- Threatened people try to reframe evidence so that those who had generated the emotion will come to doubt their reality.

Emotional Inertia Rule: (Pages 43-54)

- Emotional states only change when acted upon by a change in thought. (Emotions at rest remain at rest; Emotions in motion remain in motion.)

Emotional Value Rule (Pages 21-23)
- Emotions are not right, wrong, good, bad, positive or negative.
- Behavior (which can be right, wrong, positive or negative) dictates an emotion's relative value.

Emotional Being Rule (Pages 17-18)
- For every emotion a human can name, one hundred thousand people exist right now who truly believe they are that emotion.*
- For every person who believes they are the emotion that they experience, there are at least two other people who know better.*
- For every human being who believes they are an emotion, there was at least one other person who somehow conveyed to them the idea that this was true.
- **Examples:** I am angry, sad, mad, glad, or happy.

Emotional Transformation Rule: (Pages 32, 39, 105, 108, 110, **113**, 115, 116, 117)
- Thoughts create and transform emotions.

Exploration Opportunity:

1. What rules can you come up with regarding insights you gathered from this book?

2. Write them out!

* **Humor Moment:** *There's no scientific basis for this; it just sounds funny enough to be true!*

B. Ed's Words

Ed has been very kind to share some of his words and phrases here with you. Take some time to review them and decide for yourself what the true emotion is when Ed's words or phrases come to visit you.

...

Abandoned	Adulterated	To	tempered	Besieged
Abashed	Advanced	Appalled	Badgered	Besmirched
Abducted	Affected	Appealed	Baffled	Betrayed
Abhorred	Affirmed	Appeased	Baited	Bewildered
Absent	Afflicted	Applauded	Balanced	Bewitched
Minded	Affrayed	Appraised	Bamboozled	Biased
Absolved	Affronted	Appreciated	Banished	Big Hearted
Absorbed	Aggravated	Approved	Banned	Bitched At
Abstracted	Aggrieved	Approved Of	Bantered	Blackened
Abused	Agitated	Argued With	Barracked	Blacklisted
Accelerated	Agonized	Aroused	Barraged	Blackmailed
Accepted	Ailed	Ashamed	Barred	Blamed
Acclaimed	Alarmed	Asphyxiated	Battered	Blanketed
Acclimated	Alienated	Assaulted	Battered	Blasted
Accom-	Allied	Assessed	About	Blessed
modated	Allowed	Assuaged	Bawled Out	Blighted
Accomp-	Allured	Assured	Beckoned	Blocked
lished	Amazed	Astonished	Bedazzled	Bloodied
Accosted	Ambushed	Astounded	Bedeviled	Bloomed
Accredited	Amused	Atrophied	Befriended	Blossomed
Accused	Analyzed	Attached	Befuddled	Bludgeoned
Acknow-	Anchored	Attacked	Begged	Blurred
ledged	Anesthetized	Attracted	Beguiled	Boggled
Activated	Anguished	Automated	Beleaguered	Bombarded
Actualized	Animated	Avenged	Belittled	Bored
Addicted	Annihilated	Avoided	Beloved	Bossed
Admired	Annoyed	Awakened	Bemused	Around
Admonished	Antagonized	Awed	Berated	Bothered
Adored	Antiquated	Babied	Bereaved	Bowled Over
Adorned	Apologized	Bad	Beseeched	Boxed In

Uncommon Sense about Everyday Feelings

Boxed Out
Braced
Brainwashed
Branded
Bridled
Bright Eyed
Broken
 Hearted
Bruised
Brushed Off
Brutalized
Bugged
Buggered
Bullied
Bummed
Bummed
 Out
Burdened
Buried
Burned
Burned Out
Burned Up
Bushed
Bush-
 whacked
Busted
Buzzed
Bypassed
Caged
Caged In
Caged Up
Cajoled
Calmed
Calmed
 Down
Cannibalized
Capitulated
Captivated
Captured

Cared About
Carded For
Carried
Carried
 Away
Castigated
Catapulted
Categorized
Censored
Censured
Centered
Chafed
Chagrined
Chained
Challenged
Changed
Charged
Charmed
Chased
Chastised
Cheapened
Cheated
Cheated On
Cherished
Chided
Chilled
Choked
Choked Up
Chucked Out
Chuffed
Circum-
 vented
Civilized
Cleansed
Clear
 Headed
Clearheaded
Clenched
Cloistered

Closed
Closed In
Closed Out
Closed
 Minded
Clouded
Clowned
Clued In
Coaxed
Coddled
Coerced
Cold
 Blooded
Cold Hearted
Collapsed
Collected
Comforted
Commanded
Committed
Compared
Compelled
Complicated
Compli-
 mented
Composed
Compressed
Compro-
 mised
Conceited
Concentrated
Concerned
Condemned
Condescend-
 ed To
Confined
Confirmed
Conflicted
Confounded
Confronted

Confused
Connected
Conned
Conquered
Consecrated
Considered
Consoled
Conspired
 Against
Constrained
Constricted
Consulted
Consumed
Contained
Contam-
 inated
Contented
Controlled
Convicted
Convinced
Cooled
 Down
Cooled Off
Coped With
Copied
Cornered
Corralled
Corrupted
Coveted
Cramped
Crazed
Creeped Out
Crippled
Criticized
Crooked
Crossed
Crowded
Crucified
Crumpled

Crushed
Cuckolded
Cuddled
Culled
Cultivated
Cultured
Cursed
Damaged
Damned
Dared
Dashed
Daunted
Dazed
Deafened
Debased
Debated
Debauched
Debilitated
Deceived
Decided
Decimated
Dedicated
Defamed
Defeated
Defiled
Defined
Deflated
Deformed
Degraded
Dehuman-
 ized
Dejected
Delayed
Deleted
Delighted
Delivered
Deluded
Demeaned
Demented

Demolished	Dignified	Disinclined	Domineered	Embittered
Demonized	Diminished	Disinterested	Doomed	Emerged
Demoralized	Disabled	Disjointed	Doped	Emotionally
Demoted	Disaffected	Disliked	Doted On	Bloated
Demotivated	Disappointed	Dislocated	Double	Emotionally
Denatured	Disapproved	Dislodged	Crossed	Constipated
Denigrated	Of	Dismayed	Doubted	Empowered
Denounced	Disbelieved	Dismissed	Down-	Enabled
De-nurtured	Discarded	Disobeyed	hearted	Enamored
Depended	Disciplined	Disorganized	Down	Enchanted
Upon	Discom-	Disoriented	Played	Enclosed
Depleted	bobulated	Disowned	Dragged	Encom-
Deported	Disconcerted	Disparaged	Drained	passed
Depraved	Disconnect-	Dispirited	Dreaded	Encouraged
Deprecated	ed	Displaced	Dried Out	Encroached
Depreciated	Discontented	Displeased	Dried Up	Upon
Depressed	Discounted	Dispossessed	Dropped	Encumbered
Deprived	Discouraged	Disputed	Drowned	Endangered
Derailed	Discredited	Disquieted	Drummed	Endowed
Derided	Discrimi-	Disregarded	Dulled	Endured
Desecrated	nated	Disrespected	Dumb-	Energized
Deserted	Disdained	Dissatisfied	Founded	Enervated
Desiccated	Disembodied	Dissected	Dumbed	Engaged
Desired	Disem-	Dissed	Down	Engrossed
Despised	powered	Dissipated	Dumped	Engulfed
Destroyed	Dis-	Dissociated	Dumped On	Enhanced
Detached	enchanted	Distorted	Duped	Enlightened
Detained	Disen-	Distracted	Dwarfed	Enlivened
Deteriorated	franchised	Distressed	Eased	Enmeshed
Determined	Disentangled	Distrusted	Eclipsed	Ennobled
Detested	Disfavored	Disturbed	Edified	Enraged
Detoxified	Disgraced	Disused	Educated	Enraptured
Devalued	Disgruntled	Diverted	Effaced	Enriched
Devastated	Disguised	Divided	Elated	Enslaved
Devoted	Disgusted	Divorced	Electrified	Entangled
Devoured	Disheartened	Dogged	Elevated	Entertained
Diagnosed	Disheveled	Domesti-	Emancipated	Enthralled
Dictated To	Dishonored	cated	Emasculated	Enticed
Diffused	Disillusioned	Dominated	Embarrassed	Entitled

Uncommon Sense about Everyday Feelings

Entombed
Entranced
Entrapped
Entrenched
Entrusted
Envied
Equipped
Eradicated
Erased
Escalated
Established
Esteemed
Estranged
Evaded
Evaluated
Even
  Tempered
Evicted
Eviscerated
Exacerbated
Exalted
Examined
Exasperated
Excited
Excluded
Excoriated
Exculpated
Excused
Execrated
Exempted
Exhausted
Exhilarated
Exiled
Exonerated
Exorcised
Experienced
Exploited
Exposed
Expunged

Extricated
Extroverted
Fainthearted
Fair Minded
Falsely
  Accused
Famished
Fascinated
Fathered
Fatigued
Favored
Fawned
Fawned
  Over
Fazed
Feared
Fettered
Finished
Fired
Fixated
Flabber-
  gasted
Flagellated
Flattered
Flawed
Fleeced
Flim-
  flammed
Flipped Out
Flogged
Floored
Flummoxed
Flustered
Focused
Fogged In
Foiled
Followed
Forced
Fore Sighted

Formed
Fortified
Fouled
Fouled Up
Frayed
Fractured
Fragmented
Framed
Frazzled
Freaked
Freaked Out
Frenzied
Fret Filled
Fried
Fried Up
Frightened
Frustrated
Fulfilled
Gagged
Galled
Galvanized
Garbled
Gifted
Gilded
Glamorized
Goaded
Gob
  Smacked
Good
  Hearted
Good
  Mannered
Good
  Natured
Graded
Granted
Gratified
Grieved
Grossed Out

Grounded
Guarded
Guided
Guilt
  Tripped
Gutted
Gypped
Haggled
Hallowed
Hammered
Hampered
Handicapped
Harangued
Harassed
Hard Headed
Hard
  Hearted
Hard Pressed
Hardened
Harnessed
Harried
Hassled
Hated
Haunted
Healed
Heartened
Heavy
  Hearted
Heckled
Heeded
Helped
Hen Pecked
Herded
High Pitched
High
  Spirited
Hindered
Hoaxed
Honored

Hoodwinked
Horrified
Hot Headed
Hot
  Tempered
Hounded
Humbled
Humiliated
Humored
Hunted
Hurried
Hushed
Hustled
Hyped Up
Hypnotized
Idolized
Ignored
Ill Humored
Ill Tempered
Illuminated
Imbalanced
Immobilized
Impaired
Impassioned
Impeded
Impelled
Imperiled
Imposed
  Upon
Impressed
Imprisoned
Impugned
Incapacitated
Incensed
Incon-
  venienced
Inculcated
Indebted
Indicted

Emotional Awareness *Made Easy*

Indoctrinated	Isolated	Learned	Mesmerized	Muzzled
Inebriated	Jaded	Lectured To	Messed	Mystified
Infantilized	Jaundiced	Led Astray	Around	Nagged
Infatuated	Jazzed	Level	Messed Up	Nailed
Infected	Jeered	Headed	Messed With	Narrow
Inflamed	Jeopardized	Liberated	Micro	Minded
Inflated	Jerked	Lied About	Managed	Nauseated
Influenced	Around	Lied To	Miffed	Needed
Informed	Jilted	Lifted	Minimized	Needled
Infuriated	Jinxed	Light	Mis-	Negated
Infused	Jolted	Hearted	diagnosed	Neglected
Ingratiated	Jostled	Liked	Misguided	Nestled
Inhibited	Judged	Limited	Misinformed	Nettled
Injured	Juggled	Lionhearted	Mis-	Niggled
Inoculated	Juiced	Listened To	interpreted	Nit Picked
Inspired	Juiced Up	Loathed	Misled	Nonplused
Instilled	Jumbled	Loosed	Mis-	Noticed
Insulted	Junked	Lorded Over	represented	Nourished
Integrity	Justified	Loved	Missed	Nudged
Filled	Kicked	Low Spirited	Missed Out	Nullified
Interested	Kicked	Lured	Mistreated	Numbed
Interfered	Around	Lynched	Mistrusted	Nursed
With	Kicked Back	Maimed	Misused	Obeyed
Interrelated	Kidded	Maladjusted	Mixed Up	Objectified
Interrogated	Kindhearted	Maligned	Mobilized	Obligated
Interrupted	Knocked	Mal-	Mocked	Obliged
Intimidated	Knocked	nourished	Molded	Obliterated
Intoxicated	Down	Man	Molested	Obscured
Intrigued	Knocked Out	Handled	Mollified	Observed
Introverted	Knocked Up	Managed	Monitored	Obsessed
Intruded	Knotted	Mangled	Monopolized	Obstructed
Upon	Knotted Up	Manipulated	Mortified	Offended
Inundated	Kowtowed	Marginalized	Mothered	Old
Invalidated	Labeled	Married	Motivated	Fashioned
Invigorated	Lambasted	Marshaled	Moved	One Upped
Invited	Lampooned	Around	Muddled	Open
Involved	Laughed At	Medicated	Muffled	Handed
Irked	Lavished	Melded	Mugged	Open
Irritated	Leaned On	Menaced	Mutinied	Minded

143

Uncommon Sense about Everyday Feelings

Opinionated
Opposed
Oppressed
Ordained
Organized
Orphaned
Ostracized
Ousted
Outdated
Out-numbered
Out-powered
Outraged
Outranked
Over-estimated
Overjoyed
Overloaded
Overlooked
Over-powered
Over-whelmed
Overworked
Over Protected
Over Ruled
Over Simplified
Over Depended Upon
Over Worried
Owed
Owned
Pacified
Pained
Paired

Paired Off
Paired Up
Pampered
Panicked
Paralyzed
Pardoned
Passed By
Passed Off
Passed Over
Passed Up
Patronized
Peeved
Penetrated
Perceived
Perplexed
Persecuted
Persuaded
Perturbed
Perverted
Pestered
Petered Out
Petrified
Picked Apart
Picked On
Pierced
Pigeon Holed
Pillaged
Pissed
Pissed Off
Pissed On
Pitied
Placated
Plagued
Played a Fool
Played With
Pleased
Plumbed

Plundered
Poised
Poisoned
Polished
Polluted
Pooped
Pooped on
Pooped out
Possessed
Praised
Preached To
Precluded
Preoccupied
Prepared
Pressed
Pressured
Preyed Upon
Privileged
Prized
Probationed
Probed
Progress Minded
Promised
Promoted
Pro-pagandized
Propelled
Prosecuted
Prostituted
Protected
Provoked
Psyched
Puffed Up
Pulled
Pulled Ahead
Pulled Apart
Pulled Away

Pulled Back
Pulled Down
Pulled Forward
Pulled In
Pulled Up
Pulverized
Pummeled
Pumped
Pumped Up
Punched
Punished
Purged
Pursued
Pushed
Pushed Ahead
Pushed Away
Pushed Apart
Pushed Back
Pushed Down
Pushed Forward
Pushed In
Pushed Up
Puzzled
Qualified
Quarantined
Quashed
Queried
Questioned
Quieted
Quizzed
Raided
Railroaded
Raked

Raked Over
Ransacked
Raped
Rated
Rattled
Ravished
Re-energized
Re-enforced
Reamed
Reamed Out
Reassured
Rebuffed
Rebuked
Recognized
Reconciled
Recovered
Recruited
Redeemed
Reduced
Refined
Refreshed
Refueled
Regimented
Rejected
Rejoiced
Rejuvenated
Relaxed
Released
Relieved
Remedied
Removed
Renewed
Repelled
Replaced
Replenished
Reposed
Repressed
Reprimand-ed

Reproached	Sated	Self Hatred	Snowed	Strained
Reproved	Satiated	Sentenced	Snubbed	Stranded
Repulsed	Satisfied	Separated	Snuggled	Strangled
Rescued	Saved	Settled	Soft Hearted	Strengthened
Resented	Scandalized	Shadowed	Soothed	Stressed
Reserved	Scape-	Shamed	Sophisti-	Stretched
Resigned	goated	Shaped	cated	Striped
Resolved	Scared	Shattered	Soured	Stroked
Respected	Scarred	Sheltered	Spared	Strong
Rested	Scathed	Shielded	Spirited	Armed
Restrained	Scattered	Shocked	Spoiled	Strong
Restricted	Scintillated	Short-	Spooked	Willed
Retaliated	Scoffed At	changed	Squandered	Stuffed
Retaliated	Scolded	Shouted At	Squashed	Stumped
Against	Scorned	Shredded	Squeezed	Stunned
Retarded	Screwed	Shunned	Squelched	Stunted
Retired	Screwed	Sickened	Stained	Stupefied
Reunited	Over	Side Lined	Stalked	Subdued
Revealed	Screwed Up	Silenced	Startled	Subjugated
Revered	Scrutinized	Simplified	Starved	Subordinated
Reviled	Sealed In	Singled Out	Steamed	Sucked Up
Revisited	Sealed Off	Skilled	Steamed Up	To
Revitalized	Sealed Out	Skipped	Stepped On	Suckered
Revived	Sealed Up	Slandered	Stepped	Suffocated
Revolted	Seared	Slaughtered	Over	Sullied
Rewarded	Second	Sledged	Stereotyped	Superseded
Ridiculed	Guessed	Slighted	Stifled	Supported
Riled	Seduced	Sloshed	Stigmatized	Suppressed
Riveted	Seized	Slugged	Stilted	Surpassed
Roasted	Selected	Smacked	Stimulated	Surprised
Robbed	Self	Smacked	Stirred	Surrendered
Ruffled	Absorbed	Down	Stirred Up	Surveyed
Ruined	Self Assured	Smashed	Stomped On	Suspended
Ruled	Self	Smoked	Stoned	Swamped
Rushed	Centered	Smothered	Stonewalled	Swindled
Sabotaged	Self	Smudged	Stout	Switched On
Sacrificed	Disciplined	Snapped At	Hearted	Talked
Sanctified	Self	Snarled At	Straight	About
Sanctioned	Expressed	Snookered	Laced	Talked At

Talked To	Tossed	About	Unloved	Well
Talked With	Tossed	Under	Unsupported	Rounded
Teased	About	Protected	Un-trusted	Whelmed
Terrified	Trapped	Under Used	Unwanted	Wicked
Threatened	Troubled	Under	Used	Wide Eyed
Thwarted	Tuckered	Estimated	Used Up	Worried
Tired	Tuckered Out	Uninformed	Violated	
Tired Out	Uncared	Uninterested	Vindicated	

Exploration Opportunity:

1. Identify the emotion behind each of the words above.
   a. **Example***: Abused → Hurt*

2. For every emotion you identify in turn identify the type of emotion it is.
   a. **Example***: Hurt → Pain Emotion*

C. Multi Word Emotional Expressions

Which of these phrases are genuine emotions? Which of these
word combinations are judgments? Which are or can be moods?
(*See page 54 for mood overview*)

...

Above Average	Broken Up	Gob Stricken
Accident Prone	Brow Beaten	Good Looking
At a Loss	Cast About	Good Will
At Ease	Cast Out	Goose Bumpy
At Home	Clung To	Grief Stricken
At Peace	Cold Feet	Grown Up
At Peril	Cold Heart	Guilt Free
At Rest	Cold Sweat	Gut Reaction
At Risk	Cut Down	Happy-Go-Lucky
At War	Cut Off	Hard Working
Awe Struck	Devoid of.any..	Health Conscious
Battle Fatigued	Down & Out	Heart Full
Battle Weary	Down in the Dumps	Heart to Heart
Battle Worn	Drawn Away	Held Dear
Beaten Down	Drawn Back	High Pitch
Below Average	Drawn In	Horror Stricken
Blame Free	Drawn Toward	Hot to Trot
Blown Apart	Easy Going	Hung Out
Blown Around	Emotionally	Hung Over
Blown Away	Bankrupt	Hung Up
Blown Over	Empty of...	Hunky Dory
Blown to Bits	Fed Up	Hyper-vigilant
Blown to Pieces	First Class	Ill at Ease
Blown Up	First Rate	In a Fix
Blue Funk	Fraternal Loyalty	In a Huff
Bound Up	Full of ...	In a Quandary
Brain Washable	Full of Life	In a Stew
Breath Taken	Full On	In Alignment
Broken Down	Fun Loving	In Control

147

Uncommon Sense about Everyday Feelings

In Despair	Out of Place	Self-Hating
In Doubt	Out of Sorts	Self Indulgent
In Fear	Out of Style	Self-Knowing
In Harmony	Out of Touch	Self Loathing
In Pain	Out of Tune	Self Love
In the Dumps	Out Reasoned	Self Pity
In the Way	Over Controlled	Self-Pitying
In Touch/Tune	Over Done	Self-Pleasing
Inside Out	Paid Off	Self-Reflective
Kept at Bay	Prone To	Self-Rejection
Kept Away	Puppy Love	Self Reliant
Kept In	Put Away	Self Righteous
Kept Out	Put Down	Self-Sacrificing
Lagging Behind	Put On	Self-Serving
Laid Back	Put Out	Self Understanding
Lament Full	Put Upon	Set Up
Law Abiding	Red Hot	Set Upon
Left Out	Riding High	Shook Out
Let Down/Go	Robot Like	Shook Up
Love Sick/Struck	Run Down	Shot Down
Mad For	Run Out	Shut In
Made Fun of	Run Over	Shut Out
Maternal Loyalty	Second Class	Sick at Heart
Missing Out	Second Rate	Slap Happy
Nit Picking	Self-Acceptance	Smart-Alecky
Nit Picky	Self-Acceptant	Soft Spoken
Off the Hook	Self-Aggrandizing	Soft Spot
On Call	Self Confident	Sold Out
On Display	Self-Conscious	Struck Down
On Hold	Self-Deprecating	Stuck Up
On the Side	Self-Depreciating	Torn Apart
On Time	Self Destructive	Torn Up
Out of Balance	Self-Effacing	Under The Weather
Out of Control	Self-Flagellating	Wild About
Out of It	Self-Forgiving	Wild For
Out of Luck	Self Hate	Worn out

D. Quiz Yourself!

The following is a list of words* people use to express emotions. You may want to explore it to see what messages you can find. Which words can you identify as genuine emotions and which words are judgments? What messages become clear once you examine each?

* All *"bolded"* words already have corresponding descriptions within this book.

...

Aback	Accosting	Adverse	Ail	Amore
Aberrant	Accountable	Affable	Aimless	Amorous
Aberration	Accurate	Affect	Airy	Amorousness
Abhor	Accusatory	Affection	**Alarm**	Amour
Abhorrent	Accusing	Affectionate	Alert	Amusement
Abhorrence	Acerbic	Affectivity	Alertness	Amusing
Abject	Aching	**Affinity**	Alien	Anarchistic
Ablaze	Acquiescent	Affirmative	Alive	Ancient
Able	Acquisitive	Affluent	Allegiance	Anemic
Abnormal	Acrimonious	Affray	Allowing	**Anger**
Abominable	Active	Aflutter	Alluring	Angry
Abrasive	Acuteness	Afraid	Almighty	**Angst**
Absorbent	Adamant	Against	Alone	**Anguish**
Abstemious	Adaptable	**Agape**	Aloof	**Animosity**
Abstract	Adept	**Aggression**	Alright	**Annoyance**
Absurd	Adequate	Aggressive	Altruistic	Annoying
Abundant	Admirable	**Aghast**	Amateur	Anonymous
Abusive	**Admiration**	Agile	Amazing	Antagonistic
Abysmal	Admiring	Agitation	Ambiguous	Anticipation
Abyssal	Adorable	Aglow	Ambitious	**Antipathy**
Acceptable	Adoring	Agnostic	**Ambivalence**	Antisocial
Acceptance	Adrift	Agog	Ambivalent	Antsy
Accepting	Adroit	**Agony**	Amenable	Anxiety
Accessible	Adulation	Agoraphobic	Amiable	**Anxious**
Accom-	Adult	Agreeable	Amicable	Apart
modating	Adventurous	Ahead	Amity	Apathetic

149

Uncommon Sense about Everyday Feelings

Apathy	**Attraction**	Beaten	Blind	Brisk
Apologetic	Attractive	Beatific	Bliss	Bristling
Apoplectic	Atypical	Beautiful	Blissful	Broad
Appeal	Audacious	Beggarly	Blithe	Broken
Appealing	Austere	Behavior	Bloody	Brooding
Appreciation	Authentic	Behind	Blooming	Broody
Appreciative	Authoritarian	Beholden	Blossoming	Brutal
Apprehen-	Authoritative	Believable	Blue	Bubbly
sion	Autocratic	Bellicose	Blur	Bullish
Apprehensive	Automatic	Belligerent	Blurry	Bumpy
Approachable	Autonomous	Belonging	Blushing	Buoyant
Appropriate	Available	Beneficent	Boastful	Burdensome
Aquiver	Avaricious	Benevolent	Bodacious	Bursting
Archaic	Average	Benign	Bogus	Busy
Ardency	Aversive	Bent	Boiling	Butterflies
Ardent	Avid	Bereft	Boisterous	Calculating
Ardor	Avoiding	Berserk	Bold	Callous
Argumenta-	Awake	Beset	Boldness	Callow
tive	Aware	Bestial	Bombastic	Calm
Aristocratic	**Awe**	Better	Bonkers	Calmness
Arrogance	Awesome	Bewitching	**Boredom**	Candid
Arrogant	Awestruck	Big	Boring	Canny
Artful	Awful	Bilious	Bossy	Cantankerous
Articulate	**Awkward**	Bitchy	Bother	Capable
Artificial	Awry	Biting	Bothersome	Capacity
Artistic	Babyish	Bitter	Bought	Capitulating
Artless	Backward	Bitterness	Bouncy	Capitulation
Ascetic	Bad	Bizarre	Bound	Capricious
Asinine	Ballistic	Black	Brainy	Captious
Asleep	Banal	Blah	Brash	Captivating
Asocial	Bankrupt	Blameless	Bratty	Captive
Assertive	Bare	Blaming	Brave	Care
Astonish	Barren	Bland	Brazen	Carefree
Astute	Base	Blank	Breakable	Careful
Asymmetrical	Bashful	Blasé	Breathless	Careless
Athletic	Bearable	Blasphemous	Breezy	Careworn
Atrocious	Bearish	Bleak	Brief	Caring
Attachment	Beastly	Bled	Bright	Case
Attentive	Beat	Bleeding	Brilliant	Cast

Casual
Catatonic
Catty
Caught
Cautious
Cavalier
Cerebral
Certain
Chagrin
Challenging
Changing
Chaotic
Charismatic
Charitable
Charming
Chaste
Chatty
Cheap
Cheeky
Cheerful
Cheerless
Cheery
Cherishing
Chic
Chicken
Childish
Childlike
Chilly
Chipper
Chivalrous
Chosen
Chubby
Churlish
Circumspect
Civil
Classy
Claustropho-
  bic
Clean

Clear
Clever
Clingy
Close
Closeness
Cloudy
Clueless
Clumsy
Coarse
Cocky
Codependent
Cognizant
Cold
Coldness
Collapsing
Colorful
Colossal
Comatose
Combative
Comedic
Comely
Comfort
Comfortable
Comfy
Commanding
Commend-
  able
Common
Common-
  place
Commotion
Communica-
  tive
Companion-
  able
Comparative
Compassion
Compassion-
  ate

Compatible
Competence
Competent
Competitive
Complacent
Complaint
Complement-
  ary
Complete
Completion
Complex
Compliant
Compliment-
  ary
Composure
Compro-
  mising
Compulsive
Compunction
Concentration
Concern
Conciliatory
Concise
Condescen-
  ding
Conditional
Confidence
Confident
Confirming
Conforming
Confronting
Confrontive
Confusion
Congenial
Conniving
Conscientious
Conscious
Conservative
Considerate

Consistent
Consoling
Conspicuous
Conspiratorial
Constant
**Consterna-
  tion**
Constraint
Constructive
Consummate
Contagious
Contemp-
  lative
Contempt
Contemptible
Contemp-
  tuous
Content
Contentious
Contentment
Contradictory
Contrary
Contributing
Contrite
Controlling
Convenient
Conventional
Convincing
Convivial
Convulsive
Cooing
Cool
Cooperative
Copasetic
Coping
Cordial
Correct
Corrosive
Corrupt

Counterfeit
Courage
Courageous
Courteous
Courtly
Covetous
Cowardice
Cowardly
Coy
Cozy
Crabby
Crafty
Cranky
Crap
Crappy
Crash
Crass
Craving
Crazy
Creative
Credible
Credulous
Creeps
Creepy
Crestfallen
Criminal
Critical
Cross
Crotchety
Cruddy
Crude
Cruel
Cruelty
Crummy
Crush
Cryptic
Cuckoo
Cuddly
Culpable

Cultivation	Deficient	Desultory	Discontent-	Distrust
Culture	Definite	Detachment	ment	Distrustful
Cumbersome	Degenerate	Determination	Discovery	Disturbance
Cunning	Degradation	Detest	Discreet	Dizzy
Cupidity	**Déjà Vu**	Detestable	Discrete	Docile
Curious	Dejection	Deviant	Discrimin-	Dogmatic
Curiosity	Delectable	Devious	ating	Doleful
Curly	Deleterious	Devoid	Discrimin-	Domestic
Curmudge-	Deliberate	Devotedness	ation	Dominant
only	Delicacy	Devotion	Disdain	Dominating
Cut	Delicate	Devout	Disdainful	Domineering
Cute	Delicious	Dictatorial	**Disgust**	Done
Cynical	**Delight**	Different	Disgusting	Dorky
Daffy	Delightful	Difficult	Disharmon-	Doting
Dainty	Delinquent	Diffident	ious	Doubt
Damp	Delirious	Diligent	Dishonest	**Doubtful**
Dangerous	Demanding	Dim	Dishonorable	Dowdy
Daring	Democratic	Dimension-	Disingenuous	Down
Dark	Demure	less	Disinterest	Downcast
Dashing	Dense	Diminutive	**Dislike**	Downtrodden
Daunting	Dependable	Diplomatic	Disloyal	Drab
Dauntless	Dependent	Dire	Dismal	Drama
Dead	**Depression**	Direct	Dismay	Dramatic
Deafening	Depth	Directionless	Dismissive	Drastic
Dear	Derisive	Dirty	Disobedient	**Dread**
Debonair	Deserving	Disagreeable	Disorderly	Dreadful
Decadent	Desirable	Disappointing	Dispassionate	Dreamy
Deceitful	**Desire**	**Disappoint-**	Dispensable	Dreary
Decent	Desirous	**ment**	Disposable	Drive
Deceptive	Desolate	Disapproving	Disquiet	Driven
Decisive	Desolation	Disarming	Disrespect	Droopy
Decrepit	**Despair**	Disbelieving	Disruptive	Drowning
Deep	Despairing	Discard-able	Dissident	Drunk
Deepness	Desperate	Discerning	Distance	Dry
Defective	Despicable	Discernment	Distant	Dubious
Defenseless	Despondency	Discomfit	Distinct	Dull
Defensive	Despondent	**Discomfort**	Distinctive	Dumb
Deferent	Destitute	Disconsolate	Distraught	Dusty
Defiant	Destructive	Discontent	Distress	Dutiful

Emotional Awareness *Made Easy*

Dynamic	Emotive	Evasive	Fallen	Ferocity
Dysfunctional	Empathetic	Evil	Fallible	Fertile
Eager	Empathic	Exacerbating	Fallow	Fervency
Early	**Empathy**	Exact	Falsely	Fervent
Earnest	Emphasis	Exasperating	Faltering	Fervor
Earnestness	Emphatic	**Exasperation**	Familiarity	Festive
Earthy	Empty	Excellent	Famous	Few
Easy	Enchanting	Excess	Fanatical	Fickle
Ebullient	Enchantment	Excessive	Fanaticism	Fidelity
Eccentric	Encouraging	Excitability	Fanciful	Fidgety
Eclectic	Endearment	Excitable	**Fancy**	Fiendish
Economical	Enduring	Excitement	Fantabulous	Fierce
Ecstasy	Energetic	Exempt	Fantasizing	Fierceness
Ecstatic	Energy	Exhaustion	Fantastic	Fiery
Edgy	Engaging	Exigent	Farcical	Filthy
Edifying	Enigmatic	Exotic	Fascinating	Fine
Effective	Enjoyment	Expansive	Fascination	Finicky
Effeminate	**Enmity**	Expectant	Fashionable	Fire
Effervescent	**Ennui**	Expectation	Fast	Firm
Effete	Enterprising	Experimental	Fastidious	First
Efficacious	Entertaining	Exploitative	Fat	Fit
Efficient	**Enthusiasm**	Explosive	Fatalistic	Flaky
Effort	Enthusiastic	Expressive	Fatherless	Flamboyant
Effusive	Enticing	Extraordinary	Fatherly	Flame
Egocentric	Entre-	Extravagant	Fatuous	Flammable
Egotistic	preneurial	Extreme	Fawning	Flappable
Egotistical	Envious	Extremity	**Fear**	Flat
Elastic	**Envy**	Exuberant	Fearful	Fledgling
Elation	**Epicaricacy**	Exultant	Fearless	Flexible
Elderly	Equal	Fabulous	Feckless	Flighty
Electric	Equality	Facetious	Feeble	Flimsy
Elegant	Equitable	Factious	Feeling	Flip
Eloquent	Erasable	Faculty	Feisty	Flippant
Elusive	Eros	Faint	Felicitous	Flirtatious
Embarrass-	Essential	Fair	Feminine	Floundering
ment	Ethereal	**Faith**	Ferment	Flourishing
Eminent	Ethical	Faithful	Fermenting	Fluffy
Emotional	Euphoria	Faithless	Ferocious	Fluid
Emotionless	Euphoric	Fake	Ferociousness	Flush

Uncommon Sense about Everyday Feelings

Fluttering
Foggy
Fond
Fondness
Foolhardy
Foolish
Forbearance
Forbearing
Forbidden
Force
Forceful
Forcefulness
Foreign
Forgetful
Forgettable
Forgivable
Forgiven
Forgiveness
Forgiving
Forgotten
Forlorn
Formidable
Forsaken
Forthright
Fortunate
Forward
Foul
Fragile
Frail
Frank
Frantic
Fraternal
Fraudulent
Freakish
Freaky
Free
Frenetic
Fresh
Fretful

Fretting
Friendless
Friendliness
Friendly
Friendship
Fright
Frigid
Frisky
Frivolous
Frolicsome
Frowning
Frugal
Fruitful
Frustration
Full
Fuming
Fun
Functional
Funky
Funny
Furious
Fury
Fussy
Futile
Fuzzy
Gain
Gallant
Game
Gauche
Gaudy
Gawky
Gay
Generosity
Generous
Genial
Gentile
Gentle
Genuine
Ghastly

Giant
Giddy
Gigantic
Giggly
Giving
Glad
Gladness
Glamorous
Gleaming
Glee
Gleeful
Glib
Gloom
Gloomy
Glorious
Glowing
Glum
Gluttonous
Gnawing
Godly
Good
Goofy
Gorgeous
Gory
Gothic
Graceful
Gracious
Grand
Grandiose
Grateful
Gratitude
Grave
Greasy
Great
Greed
Greedy
Gregarious
Grey
Grief

Grieving
Grim
Groovy
Gross
Grotesque
Grouchy
Groveling
Grown
Grubby
Grumpy
Guilt
Guiltless
Guilty
Gullible
Gushy
Gutless
Gutsy
Haggard
Handsome
Handy
Hankering
Hapless
Happiness
Happy
Hard
Hardy
Harmless
Harmonious
Harsh
Hasty
Hate
Hateful
Hatred
Haughty
Hazy
Headstrong
Heady
Healthy
Heard

Heart
Heartbroken
Heartless
Heartsick
Hearty
Heat
Heavenly
Heavy
Hedonic
Heedful
Helpful
Helpless
Heroic
Hesitant
Hideous
High
Hilarious
Hissing
Hollow
Homeless
Homely
Homesick
Homesickness
Honest
Honor
Honorable
Hope
Hopeful
Hopeless
Hormonal
Horny
Horrendous
Horrible
Horrific
Horror
Hospitable
Hostile
Hostility
Hot

Huge	Impatient	ness	Infantile	Intense
Humane	Impeccable	Inconceivable	Infatuation	Intenseness
Humble	Imperfect	Inconclusive	Inferior	Intensity
Humiliation	Imperious	Incongruent	Infirm	Intent
Humility	Impermanent	Inconsiderate	Inflammatory	Interest
Humorous	Impermeable	Inconsistent	Inflexible	Interesting
Hunger	Impertinent	Inconsolable	Influential	Interfering
Hungry	Imperturbable	Inconspicuous	Ingenious	Intimate
Hurt	Impervious	Inconvenient	Ingenuous	Intimidating
Husky	Impetuous	Incorrect	Ingratiating	Intolerant
Hyper	Impious	Incorrigible	Inhospitable	Intrepid
Hyperactive	Impish	Incredible	Inhumane	Introspective
Hypocritical	Implacable	Incredulous	Inimical	Intrusive
Hysteria	Impolite	Indecent	Innocence	Intuition
Hysterical	Important	Indecision	Innocent	Intuitive
Icy	Importunate	Indecisive	Innovative	Invalidating
Idealistic	Imposing	Indefinite	Inquiring	Inventive
Idiosyncratic	Impossible	Independence	Inquisitive	Invisible
Idiotic	Impotent	Independent	Insane	Inviting
Idle	Impractical	Indescribable	Insatiable	Involvement
Idolatry	Impression	Indestructible	Inscrutable	Invulnerable
Ignoble	Impressive	Indifference	Insecure	Irascible
Ignominious	Impudent	Indifferent	Insensibility	Irate
Ignorant	Impulsive	Indignant	Insensitive	Irrational
Ill	Impure	**Indignation**	Insightful	Irreligious
Illicit	Inaccessible	Indirect	Insignificant	Irreproach-
Imagination	Inactive	Indiscreet	Insincere	able
Imaginative	Inadequacy	Indolent	Insistent	Irresistible
Immaculate	**Inadequate**	Indulgent	Insolent	Irresolute
Immature	Inane	Industrious	Insouciant	Irresponsible
Immense	Inappropriate	Ineffective	Inspiration	Irreverent
Immobile	Inattentive	Ineffectual	Instructive	Irritability
Immodest	Incapable	Inefficient	Insufficient	Irritable
Immoral	Inclination	Inept	Insulting	Irritation
Immortal	Incoherent	Inequality	Insurgent	Itchy
Immune	Incompetence	Inert	Intact	Jaunty
Impartial	Incompetent	Inexplicable	Intellectual	**Jealous**
Impassive	Incomplete	Infallible	Intelligence	Jealousy
Impatience	Incomplete-	Infamous	Intelligent	Jitters

155

Uncommon Sense about Everyday Feelings

Jittery	Languid	**Lonely**	**Malice**	Messy
Jocular	Languishing	Lonesome	Malicious	Methodical
Jolly	Languor	**Long**	Malignant	Meticulous
Jovial	Large	Longing	Malleable	Might
Joy	Lascivious	Loopy	Mammoth	Mighty
Joyful	Late	Loose	Manageable	Mild
Joyless	Laudable	Loss	Managerial	Militant
Joyous	Laughable	Lost	Maniacal	Mindful
Jubilant	Lax	Loud	Manic	Miniature
Judgment	Lazy	Lousy	Manipulative	Miraculous
Judgmental	Leaning	Lovable	Manly	Mirthful
Judicious	Lecherous	**Love**	Marauding	Misanthropic
Juicy	Leery	Loveless	Marvelous	Mischievous
Jumpy	Legitimate	Lovely	Masochistic	Miserable
Junk	Lenient	Loving	Massive	Miserly
Junky	Lethargic	Low	Masterful	**Misery**
Just	Lewd	Lowly	Masterly	Misgiving
Keen	Liable	Lowness	Materialistic	Missing
Keenness	Liberal	Loyal	Maternal	Mistaken
Kept	Licentious	Lubricious	Mature	Mistrustful
Kind	Lifeless	Lucid	Maudlin	Misty
Kindly	Lifelike	Luckless	Meager	Misunder-
Kindness	Light	Lucky	Mean	stood
Kingly	Likable	Ludicrous	Meanness	Moaning
Kinky	**Like**	Luminous	Mechanical	Mocking
Kissable	Likeable	Luring	Mediocre	Moderate
Knightly	Liking	Lurking	Meditative	Modern
Knowing	Limerence	**Lust**	Meek	Modest
Knowledge-	Limp	Lustful	Megalo-	Modesty
able	Listless	Lusty	maniacal	Monstrous
Known	Litigious	Macho	Melancholic	Moody
Kooky	Little	Mad	**Melancholy**	Mope-y
Labile	Lively	Magical	Mellow	Moping
Lackadaisical	Livid	Magnetic	Melodic	Moral
Lacking	**Loath**	Magnificent	Melodramatic	Moralistic
Lackluster	Loathing	Magnitude	Menacing	Morbid
Laconic	Loathsome	Malaise	Merciful	Mordant
Lame	Logical	Malcontent	Meritorious	Moribund
Lamenting	Loneliness	Malevolent	**Merry**	Moronic

Emotional Awareness _Made Easy_

Morose
Mothering
Motherless
Motherly
Motionless
Mournful
Mourning
Mouthy
Muddy
Mushy
Musical
Mute
Mutinous
Mysterious
Mystery
Mystical
Naïve
Naked
Nameless
Narcissistic
Narrow
Nasty
Natural
Naughty
Neat
Necessary
Needy
Negative
Negligent
Neighborly
Nervous
Nervousness
Nervy
Neurotic
Neutral
New
Nice
Nifty
Niggardly

Nihilistic
Nimble
Nitwitty
Noble
Noisy
Nomadic
Nonchalant
Noncommittal
Nonconform-
    ing
Nonexistent
Normal
Nosey
Nostalgic
Nosy
Nothing
Nourishing
Null
Numb
Numbness
Numerous
Nurturing
Nutritious
Nuts
Nutty
Obedient
Obligation
Obliging
Oblivious
Obnoxious
Obscene
Obsequious
Observant
Obsessive
Obstinate
Obvious
Odd
Off
Offensive

Officious
Ogre-ish
Okay
Old
Omnipotent
On
Open
Opportunistic
Opposition
Oppositional
Optimism
Optimist
Optimistic
Opulent
Orderly
Ordinary
Original
Ornery
Ostentation
Ostentatious
Outdone
Outgoing
Outlandish
Outrageous
Outspoken
Outstanding
Over
Overanxious
Overbearing
Overcome
Overdrawn
Oversensitive
Overwhelm
Overwrought
Overzealous
Owing
Ownership
Owning
Pain

Painful
Palpability
Palpitation
Panic
Panicky
Paranoia
Paranoid
Parasitic
Parsimonious
Partial
Partiality
Passion
Passionate
Passive
Pastoral
Paternal
Pathetic
Pathos
Patience
Patient
Peace
Peaceful
Peachy
Peck-ish
Peculiar
Pedantic
Pedestrian
Peevish
Penetrable
Pensive
Peppy
Perceptive
Peremptory
Perfect
Perfectionism
Perfectionist
Perfectionistic
Perilous
Peripheral

Perky
Permanent
Permeable
Permission
Persevering
Persistent
Persnickety
Personable
Perspicuous
Persuasive
Pert
Pertinacious
Pertinent
Perturbation
Pervious
Pessimism
Pessimist
Pessimistic
Petite
Petty
Petulant
Philanthropic
Philosophical
Phlegmatic
Phobia
Phony
Piety
Pillaging
Pious
Piss-y
Piteous
Pitiful
Pitiless
Pity
Placid
Plain
Plan-less
Playful
Pleading

Uncommon Sense about Everyday Feelings

Pleasant	Prim	Psychopathic	Rapid	Reject-able
Pleasure	Primal	Psychotic	Rapt	Rejecting
Pliable	Primary	Puerile	**Rapture**	Rejoicing
Pliant	Primitive	Punctual	Rapturous	Relaxation
Plundering	Prissy	Puny	Rare	Reliable
Plunging	Pristine	Pure	Rash	Reliant
Plush	Privacy	Purposeful	Rashness	**Relief**
Poetic	Private	Purring	Raspy	Religious
Polite	Privy	Pursuant	Rational	Relish
Pompous	Proactive	Pushy	Ratty	Reluctance
Poor	Probationary	Pusillanimity	Raunchy	Reluctant
Popular	Prodigal	Pusillanimous	Ravenous	Remarkable
Porous	Prodigious	Quaint	Ravishing	Reminiscent
Portentous	Productive	Quaking	Raw	Remiss
Posh	Profane	Qualm-ish	Reachable	**Remorse**
Positive	Professional	Quandary	Reaction	Remorseful
Possession-	Profound	Quantity	Reactionary	Remorseless
less	Progressing	Quarrelsome	Reactive	Remote
Possessive	Progressive	Queasy	Ready	Renown
Potency	Prohibition	Queer	Real	Repentance
Potent	Prolific	Querulous	Realistic	Repentant
Pout-y	Promiscuous	Questioning	Reasonable	Replaceable
Power	Promotional	Quick	Rebellious	Repose
Powerful	Prompt	Quickest	Reborn	Reprehensible
Powerless	Propagan-	Quiescent	Rebounding	Repugnant
Practical	distic	Quiet	Recalcitrant	Repulsion
Pragmatic	Propensity	Quirky	Receptive	Repulsive
Precarious	Proper	Quivery	Reckless	Request
Precious	Prosaic	Quixotic	Reclusive	Resentful
Precocious	Prosperous	Quizzical	Red	**Resentment**
Predilection	Protective	Radiant	Refinement	Resilient
Preppy	Proud	Radical	Reflective	Resistant
Presentiment	Provident	**Rage**	Refusal	Resisting
Presumptuous	Provincial	Raging	Regard	Resolute
Pretentious	Provisional	Rainy	Regressing	Resonant
Pretty	Provocative	Rambunctious	Regressive	Resourceful
Priceless	Prudent	Rancid	**Regret**	Respect
Prickly	Prudish	**Rancor**	Regretful	Respectful
Pride	Psychedelic	Rapacious	Regretless	Resplendent

Responsible	**Sad**	Sedate	Sheepish	Smiling
Responsive	Sadistic	Seductive	Shine	Smitten
Responsive-	**Sadness**	Seemly	Shiny	Smoggy
ness	Safe	Seething	**Shock**	Smooth
Restful	Sagacious	Selective	Short	Smug
Restive	Sage	Selfish	Shrewd	Smutty
Restless	Saintly	Selfless	Shrill	Sneaky
Retaliatory	Salacious	Self-pity	Shrunk	Snobbish
Reticent	Salty	Senile	Shrunken	Snobby
Revenge	Sanctifying	Sensation	Shy	Snoopy
Revengeful	Sanctimon-	Sensational	Shyness	Soaring
Reverence	ious	Sensibility	Sick	Sociable
Reverent	Sane	Sensible	Significant	Social
Revolting	Sanguine	Sensitive	Silent	Sodden
Revolutionary	Sapient	Sensitiveness	Silly	Soft
Rich	Sarcastic	Sensitivity	Simple	Softy
Ridden	Sardonic	Sensual	Sincere	Sold
Ridiculous	Sassy	Sensuous	Sinful	Solemn
Right	Sate	Sentiment	Single	Solicitous
Righteous	Satisfaction	**Sentimental**	Sinking	Solicitude
Rigid	Saucy	Sentiment-	Skank-ish	Solid
Rigorous	Savvy	ality	Skanky	Solitary
Ripe	Scandalous	Serendipitous	Skeptical	Somber
Rivalry	Scary	**Serene**	Skillful	Sophomoric
Robotic	**Schaden-**	Serious	Skinny	Sordid
Robust	**freude**	Servile	Skittish	Sore
Romantic	Scheming	Set	Slack	Sorrow
Rosy	Scholarly	Severity	Slain	Sorrowful
Rotten	Scientific	Sexual	Sleazy	Sorry
Rough	Scintillating	Sexy	Sleepy	Sough
Round	Scorn	Shaken	Sloppy	Soulful
Rowdy	Scornful	Shaky	Slothful	Sound
Rubbery	Scrawny	Shallow	Slovenly	Sour
Rude	Screeching	**Shame**	Slow	Sparkling
Rueful	Scurrilous	Shameful	Sluggish	Spartan
Ruth	Second	Shameless-	Sluttish	Spastic
Ruthless	Secondary	ness	Small	Special
Sacrificial	Secure	Sharp	Smarmy	Speechless
Sacrilegious	Security	Sharpness	Smart	Speedy

Uncommon Sense about Everyday Feelings

Spellbound	Strain	Surly	Thirsty	Unique
Spent	Strange	**Surprise**	Thorough	Unkind
Spicy	Strength	Surreal	Thoughtful	Unkindly
Spineless	Stress	Susceptible	Thoughtless	Unkindness
Spirit	Stricken	Suspending	Thrifty	Unknowing
Spiritless	Strict	Suspense	Thrill	Unknown
Spiritual	Strong	**Suspicious**	Thundering	Unruly
Spite	Struck	Swanky	Tidy	Unsafe
Spiteful	Stubborn	Sweet	Tight	Unscrupulous
Splendid	Stuck	Swell	Time	Unselfish
Splendiferous	Studious	Swift	Timidity	Unsightly
Splenetic	Stunning	Sycophantic	Tiny	Unsure
Spontaneous	Stupid	Symmetrical	Togetherness	Untrusting
Spotless	Stylish	Sympathetic	Tolerance	Unusual
Spotty	Suave	**Sympathy**	Tolerant	Upright
Sprite	Sublime	Systematic	**Torment**	Upset
Spry	Submission	Taciturn	Touchy	Uptight
Spunky	Submissive	Tactful	Tough	Useful
Square	Subordinate	Tall	Trainable	Valiant
Squealing	Subservient	Tame	**Tranquil**	Vast
Squeamish	Subtle	Tan	Tremor	Vehemence
Stable	Subversive	Tangibility	Trepidation	Verbose
Stale	Successful	Tart	Tricky	Versatile
Static	**Suffer**	Tasteless	Troubling	Vexation
Steady	Suffering	Tasty	**Trust**	**Vexatious**
Steep	Suggestion	Taunt-Able	Truthful	Vibes
Sterile	Suicidal	Teeny	Ugliest	Victorious
Stern	Sulky	Teeny-Tiny	Ugly	Vigilant
Stewing	Sullen	Tender	Uncouth	Vigor
Sticky	Sunk	Tenderness	Understand	Vigorous
Stiff	Sunny	Tense	**Understand-**	Violence
Still	Super	Tenseness	**ing**	Virtuous
Stingy	Superb	Tension	Uneasiness	Visionary
Stodgy	Supercilious	Terrible	Uneasy	Vivacious
Stoic	Superficial	Terrific	Uneven	Vociferous
Stolid	Superior	**Terror**	Unfeeling	Voiceless
Stormy	Superstitious	Testy	Unhappiness	Voluminous
Stout	Supportive	**Tetchy**	Unheard	Vulgar
Straight	Sure	Thankful	Unimportant	Vulnerability

Wandering	Wealthy	Willing	Worrisome	Yellow
Want	Weariness	Winsome	**Worry**	Yen
Warm	Weary	Wise	Worship	Young
Warmth	Weightiness	Witty	Worthy	Yummy
Warning	Wet	**Woe**	Wrath	Zany
Wasteful	Whimsical	**Wonder**	Wrong	Zeal
Watchful	Whispering	Wonderful	Xenophobic	Zealous
Watery	Wide	Wooden	Yauld	Zealousness
Weak	Wild	Worldly	**Yearn**	Zest
Weakness	Wildness	Worriment	Yearning	Zest

Exploration Opportunity:

1. Which of the above words reflect a relative intensity of an emotion? (**Example:** Voluminous) *What does each of these words tell you?*

2. Which of the above words reflect the relative absence or presence of emotion? (**Example:** Subtle) *What does each of these words tell you?*

3. Which are or can be moods? (*See page 54 for mood overview*)

E. Make the Most of This Book!

If you want to divide out the successful folks from all others, start by sorting them by the actions they take while they are learning.

Take the Challenge! Make the most of this book by doing several things to maximize the return on your investment.

Here they are:

1. **Purchase** a dependable pen, a highlighter pen and a blank notebook.
2. **Highlight** anything you read that makes sense, sparks insight for you or is usable in your business and in your life.
3. **Read** only one chapter at a time and answer the following questions about each chapter **before you proceed** to the next chapter.
   a. *What did you get from reading the chapter that you found valuable to you? Why is it valuable to you?* Please respond fully to the question! Use your notebook to record your responses. *Writing it down makes it more real.* This will give it a more fruitful impact in your life than what could occur by just thinking about it.
   b. *Write out exactly how you plan to apply what you obtained from this chapter toward your business and your life.* Please respond fully to the request! Use your notebook to record your response. Make sure you fill your plan with "*result producing*" actions and clearly defined time limits to help provoke you into action to assure your desired results.
4. Please **respond** to the three questions above and then **complete** the action items in the **Exploration** section located at the end of almost every chapter. These sections are there to help you get the most value from this book!

5. **Review** *and* **use** *the notes and action plans* in your notebook on a regular basis to *help guide you toward improving your awareness and choices.*

6. As you complete each chapter of this book, **Team up** with a trusted coach, trainer, mentor, sponsor, partner or friend to…
   a. share your responses with him or her
   b. discuss what you're getting from your reading
   c. have him or her help you refine your action plans
   d. empower him or her to help you hold yourself accountable for following through on your plans

SOME ENCOURAGEMENT TO REREAD THIS BOOK AT LEAST ONCE

The chapters of this book intertwine and build on each other. As you gain greater insight and awareness from each chapter, *chapters you have previously read will take on a different feel and reveal even more to your changing understanding.*

You'll thank yourself for doing so.

...

Invest in your education by taking <u>immediate</u> <u>action</u> on what you learn. – Coach John S. Nagy

About Dr. John S. Nagy

"Coach" Nagy is a multi-degree Professional Business and Life Coach and Technical Advisor who provides coaching support to business and career professionals throughout the world; his offices are located in the Tampa Bay area. He has run his own coaching practice since January 1989.

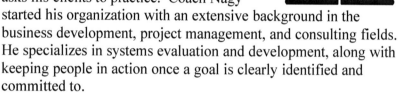

His corporation, "Coaching for Success, Inc.," operates on the same principles he asks his clients to practice. Coach Nagy started his organization with an extensive background in the business development, project management, and consulting fields. He specializes in systems evaluation and development, along with keeping people in action once a goal is clearly identified and committed to.

Dr. Nagy has a *Bachelors of Science in* Electrical Engineering and a *Masters of Science* in Engineering Management, both from the *University of South Florida.* He is an *Ordained Christian Minister* and holds a *Doctor of Ministry* from the *Lively Stone World Healing Fellowship* where he also teaches at the doctorate level.

John is also a *graduate of Coach U.* He helped spearhead the formation of the International Coaching Federation (ICF) in 1996, was *ICF's First Executive Director,* and *the co-founder and first host of The Tampa Bay Area Coaching Association.*

Coach Nagy is a well-recognized, state-certified mediator in Florida, with over a decade of experience. He mediates court-ordered cases in the 13th Judicial Circuit of Hillsborough County and trains fellow mediators in communication and mediation techniques.

John is also a columnist and published author since the early 1990's. He writes, speaks and trains others extensively on a wide variety of subjects related to personal, professional and business development – *all from a coaching prospective.* John's most recently published book was *"Provoking Success – Uncommon Coaching for the Uncommon Soul."*

Coach Nagy and his wife Candy, along with their two sons, reside in the South-Central area of Pasco County, Florida. (His sons want you to know that their dad also coaches their soccer teams every year.)